THE
REAL STEPS
TO A
REAL ESTATE
SALES CAREER

MILTON RENDELL

ABOUT THE AUTHOR

Milton Rendell commenced his career in real estate in 1987. Initially he was a sales person and within two years he was managing a sales team. In 1999, he opened his own agency with four staff and the Real Estate Plus brand was launched. Today, Real Estate Plus has multiple offices specialising in both residential and commercial real estate and the network also includes a settlement agency (Plus Your Settlements) as well as a finance broking business (Plus Loans), delivering a one stop shop.

Prior to real estate, Milton was in the finance industry and he has used what he learned from this background to help his clients. Now that doesn't mean he is boring – far from it! Milton is known for his innovation and his fun approach to marketing which has caught the attention of the media a number of times.

Milton is always challenged to improve systems and the professionalism within the industry for the benefit of clients as well his employees. He has spoken at numerous events around Australia and overseas. He has always been a student of real estate and continues to learn and keep up with the trends in the industry and share his ideas with other agents. His approach has always been to keep it simple, "a good system is one a ten year old can use!"

Known to be a true team-player, Milton sees results as a

by-product of people working together with better systems and goal-orientated approach. But he understands that to work together each of us have our own goals – personal as well as professional – which still need to be fulfilled.

Balance in life is something Milton focusses on with his staff as family is an important value. Like most, Milton has had to balance his professional life with family and being a father of four daughters life has presented him with plenty of challenges along the way.

Milton's personal mission statement is: "To have a positive influence on everyone I meet". This is something you will discover if you ever do meet him and you will find evidence of it throughout this book.

CONTENTS

INTRODUCTION

After more than 25 years of being in real estate and spending thousands of hours working with sales people in training and coaching around Australia and overseas, I thought it would be great to share some of my thoughts and observations in this book.

When I first started writing this book – just as you are reading it now – I was not sure what the outcome would be. But I did know that it was something I wanted to do and needed to do. I am now very happy it is done, and fingers crossed you will enjoy the things I have to share.

My hope is that you will take away some great information from this book that you can implement to improve your performance now and in the future. I encourage you to highlight pages and passages as you go along. There may be things you believe will help you now and others that may be useful in the future. Hopefully, this book will be an ongoing resource to help you as your career in real estate evolves and it will accompany you on your journey going forward.

Although I have attended many seminars and met and worked with some outstanding people, most of my learning has come from actually being in battle and from the mistakes I have made. You will always make mistakes but it will be what you do *after* the mistakes that matter; how you learn from that experience.

Being in sales is a lot of fun but it can bring with it some of the greatest challenges you will ever face. No matter where you are in Australia or in the world, if you are working in real estate you are dealing with people and their emotions, whether it be your boss, members of the public or your own emotions. The rules don't change, wherever you are. Handling these emotions can be challenging.

There is no quick fix to success. Yes, some people make it faster than others in this industry. These people are the great learners, students who have the ability to improve all the time. Be careful though, please do not get 'perfectionism' confused with 'better'.

Someone once told me the more you do, the luckier you become. In this book, I hope to help you create healthier habits of real estate sales success so you can become a top sales person too.

MILTON RENDELL
www.realestateplus.com.au

1. SO, YOU WANT TO BE A REAL ESTATE AGENT!

hy would you want to go into real estate? Why would any individual want to be involved in one of the greatest character-testing occupations in the world? Since having started my own career back in 1987, I have interviewed many potential sales people over the years and I am continually amazed at the variety of answers they give when I ask them the questions listed below. The top three reasons people give (which come from nearly 80% of interviewees) go something like this:

"I like people and I like houses." My response: The sad thing is just about everyone who has said this failed badly when they entered the industry.

"I've sold a few properties and I've never been that happy with the agent I had chosen, so I thought well if he/she can be making so much money not doing a lot then I must be able to

make a fortune." My response: Viewing one or two transactions doesn't make you an expert. Perhaps the agent was just very good at what he or she did and did it with a minimum of fuss, making it looked easier than it really was.

"I have always thought about going into real estate and all my friends say that I have the gift of the gab so I would be good at real estate." My response: It is good that they have actually thought about it but the fact they have the gift of the gab has little to do with real estate success. It's more about having the ability to influence people in making some of the biggest decisions in their lives that really counts.

There is a lot of emotion involved in the business of real estate and many observers do not realise some of the delicate positions that an agent deals with on a regular basis. Clients may be going through a marriage or relationship breakdown and be forced to split their assets; bereaved family members may be selling a deceased estate; vendors may be forced to sell due to financial hardship or even bankruptcy.

Then there are the smart-arses, procrastinators and the tyre-kickers who you have to deal with for weeks on end – and this is just the tip of the iceberg. Don't get me wrong, we deal with many quality people, some of whom have become my best friends, but I've had to deal with many others along the way too. And the result is the enormous fall-out of agents in the state of Western Australia where I live.

WHY DO SO MANY SALES AGENTS FAIL?

Figures show that up to 90 per cent of sales agents drop out of real estate agencies within their first 12 months. Why is this so? There are several main factors.

They don't understand what it takes to be a good agent

From an outsider's point of view, you see these people driving around in new luxury cars, dressed in smart suits and you think they must be doing well. That is because the first thing new real estate agents are told to do is to look successful. So they splash out and buy these things to impress. To find out whether they are really forging a successful career, you would be better off asking them to show you their group certificate – only that will tell the real story!

In the area where I started my career, there were 175 sales people fighting over a pie of commission generating around $5 million gross a year in fees. That meant that the average person was earning around $14,000 a year and even in 1987 that was not a lot of money. Keep in mind that these statistics meant there must have been people earning less. At the company I started with, the highest income earner had taken home $80,000 the previous year, so there was a wide range of earnings from the top to the bottom. Later I was also informed that 70 per cent of the business in the area was earned by 20 per cent of the agents, so there was not much left for the rest.

I was one of the youngest agents in my area. I was 27 years old when I started and many of the other agents were over 50 years of age. This trend has certainly changed more on the east coast of Australia than in Western Australia. I visited a successful east coast agency in 2002 (when I was 42) and I walked into an office of about 40 sales people – half of them were young enough to be my kids. A large number were in their early thirties; I did spot some grey hair but not a lot of it.

To be successful in real estate, you don't have to be in your twenties but you do need to have energy and it is your mental state rather than your age that determines your energy levels. People are attracted to enthusiastic, positive and bright people.

Before you seriously take on a role in real estate sales, it is important to understand the following:

- How you look and what car you drive is not an accurate mark of how much money you are making
- Real estate rewards are spread very thin – only a few earn the big bucks
- You will need a lot of energy and enthusiasm to succeed and you have to maintain these qualities at all times.

Don't be like the majority of people who start in the industry only to quickly find it is so different to what they expected. It's your responsibility to do your homework before committing to this industry. As you're reading this book, you're already doing well. You are obviously looking for answers.

They don't have the financial resources to stay in the industry

When you start working in real estate you need to have cash in the bank to pay the bills while you create your first sales. The fact is that you don't get paid until settlement of your first property sale. At best, this means you may get your first pay cheque approximately six to eight weeks after you start, before then you may be only on a minimum base salary. So, if you don't have at least six months of cash stored away to pay your bills, give it a miss until you have.

Barriers to entry are non-existent

Many principals (business owners) of real estate agencies will put on anyone who has a pulse (and don't tell me you haven't met an agent at least once and wondered if they really do have one). For many years, the real estate industry has been the graveyard for people who have been made redundant or turned 50 and felt the need for a change – after all, real estate might just fill that gap of time before retirement because it's really only a weekend job (their views, not mine)!

There are so many people who start working in this industry who should never have been considered for the job and that is because of the selection program that agencies have in place.

The trouble is many agencies don't have a recruitment and training program and this is why they accept just about anyone they meet. Recently I heard of no less than five agencies in our immediate area who had accepted new people to join them. I believe the number of these attending the new agents course was ten, which means at least two of these newly appointed staff would not take part in a formal training process. Maybe one or two will survive long term. This poor survival rate will be more the fault of the agency as they have probably said yes to people who should not have entered the industry. Then the potentially good ones will may get lost without guidance in the system.

Very little training (if any) is given

Just because an agent joins a franchise group doesn't mean he or she will receive good training. Training is an ongoing process not just a two-day course and hey presto you're an expert!

There are some things you just can't teach – the main one being persistence. The reason people often fail in real estate is that they simply do not persist. This is not an easy industry. For those who find the right formula and have enormous success, it is the greatest industry in the world, but for every one of them there are thousands who fail.

The initial learning curve is huge, particularly in small agencies where you find yourself answering phones when the receptionist is unavailable and undertaking duties which, in my opinion, are the biggest waste of time in the world. By agreeing to do admin duties, the principal has a back-up receptionist and hopefully someone who will do all their own paperwork too! I am not saying that you should not help out in the office, but the majority of sales people are only paid commission and therefore you need to be doing dollar-productive activities. Wouldn't you agree that it's insane for a potential $100,000 a year income-earner to do a $20,000 income-earner's task? In the end, that is exactly what you earn because you have not had the time to earn real money.

You can't sell real estate from your office desk

Representatives sit in the office and wait for the phone to ring when they should be out there generating business – it's about action not being inactive. Others burn out because they have a 'hang-around-the-office' mentality. What are they expecting? For a hundred leads to walk in?

If you are organised and qualify people well (see later chapter on prospecting) you will have plenty of great leads and won't need to hang around. Some real estate offices are places where the staff simply hang out and nobody seems to know what they are doing. Most people who fail struggle to understand that to get started they need to get moving themselves. If you are dependent on others to find your leads, you are out of the race.

Ask yourself the following question: if I was looking to sell my home, how would I find the best agent to help me? Then once you have done that, work out how you would approach that agent. When you first start in real estate sales, or if you are already in the industry, get your principal's (or boss's) attention and follow what they do. Learn about what they did when they first started and what they do now to find business.

I have been in offices where a new agent just sits around waiting for the boss to wave their magic wand and make them a great agent. It takes effort, guts and planning – something that lots of people don't have. Many who come from a nine-to-five job struggle with the concept that there is no head office to blame. The total personal accountability in real estate scares many people early and freezes them until it is only a matter of time before they leave.

Agents who fail may also blame the culture. Many struggle to understand sales culture in an office when they first start. You need to accept that there will always be greedy agents (maybe you're one of them). But keep in mind, there is always plenty of potential income out there in the field. You just have to go and find it.

They are afraid to make mistakes

I was talking to my top sales person recently about her start in the industry. She said, "Boy, did I make a lot mistakes when I started". My reply to her was, "It was great that you made lots of mistakes because that meant you were doing lots of things and therefore you learnt quickly about what to do and not to do".

Hopefully that makes sense to you. The best way not to avoid making mistakes is to not do anything. That is what many do, then they turn around and say they didn't have anyone to show them what to do. Business will come to those who look for it, not to those who wait for it and, to be honest, the latter is what many do.

One stand-out reason why many people fail is because the boss allows them to float along in the hope they may eventually find a sale. Make sure that you have a fair and tough boss who will continually test you to improve and who will spend the time to talk to you.

All of us are full of energy when we first start. It's a pity we can't bottle this energy and inject it into our bodies later on. Accept that you will make mistakes early and the more the better. Why? Because this means you are actually doing something. Show me a person who has never made a mistake and I will show you someone who has done nothing.

Mistakes are an opportunity to grow and learn. Today I'm still making mistakes and I know I will make more in the future but that's OK. If you are a perfectionist, get out now! You guys drive yourselves crazy with rules you don't need and can never expect to fulfil. Flexibility is very important. Your mind must be open to change and your ability to think on your feet is essential.

They blame the principal

Recently, I had a call from a girl who responded to an advertisement I had placed for a sales cadet. (In my business, we appoint sales cadets as personal assistants to our established reps so that they can learn the basics while being paid and eventually they become sales people themselves.) She advised me that she had started with a company three months previously and still hadn't met a licensee/ principal nor had she had one second of training. This was a franchise office. When you are green it is not easy to have the courage to approach the principal or people senior to you. But you need to and you must ask lots of questions and seek as much information as you can before you start. Question things if you have not been given training straight away because if you don't get it then, you never will.

Please don't get me wrong, there are some outstanding

companies out there. All I am suggesting is to do your homework and seek knowledge all the time. Never blame the principal because things aren't happening, it is because you have *let* this happen.

IT'S A NUMBERS GAME

Getting back to the point I made earlier about principals appointing just about anyone in the sales role, I will share with you a conversation I had with two former state managers of franchise groups. I have also heard this view expressed by a number of principals within the industry and all have responded in similar ways to the following questions: "What is your view on recruitment?" and "What should you look for in a sales person?" They have answered, "It does not matter who they are or what they do, if they can pass the course give 'em a go. The worst thing they are going to do is sell a house to their family. If they can't sell to anyone else they drop off. You know it's a numbers game and the more you have the greater chance you have."

One state manager answered, "Just throw the shit against the wall and see what sticks?"

My reply to this was, "You are joking!"

But he wasn't. He said, "Absolutely not, because it is really hard to tell who is going to be any good".

It's a sad state of affairs, isn't it? With that attitude out there it may be hard for you to find the right culture in an agency and leaders who will train you to excel. So it will come back to your attitude and how strong a goal-setter you really are (we discuss this in the next chapter) and if you understand how the industry really works. I hope this book will help.

Please don't think I am negative about the industry. I love what I do, but I am just opening your eyes to ensure you are heading in the right direction. For those who are already in the industry, you will have experienced what I am talking about or at least heard similar stories. Real estate is full of a lot of very nice people but unfortunately the successful people are few and far between. Your aim is to be one of the successful ones.

THE FIRE WITHIN

When we start a new job or project we are full of enthusiasm but in time this often wanes. Why? Do you lack interest? Are you questioning your ability to do the task or do you believe that the tasks are too difficult? We are all afraid of the unknown at times and this doubt does burn up energy. When you have negative thoughts it becomes even more difficult to cope with a new role and your doubt grows until, in your mind, it seems a hopeless endeavour.

Many of the battles we have are in our mind, so it is very important to feed our minds with the right influences at the right time and sometimes all the time. If only we could bottle that enthusiasm we started out with, then sip its power every time we needed it. But you can't so you need to control the influences of people around you, those who have the biggest effects on you, from your boss to your partner in life.

Positive people and positive influences (such as motivational books, podcasts and DVDs) will continually help to feed your fire. Never underestimate the power of the fire within. It will determine the difference between the amateur and the professional.

People can feel your fire and many are attracted to its warmth and are more than happy to help you with your goals. Success is not a journey you take alone. Along the way you will have many adventures and stories to tell but the fire will be the energy source that you will call on time and time again to move you towards your goals. You need to feed that fire, find ongoing fuel sources to increase its power and increase your learning. Your fire and passion will attract what you need to succeed so you cannot afford to let the fire die. It is easier to stoke up a fire than to create a new one. Keep your fire lit at all times and ensure there is always plenty of fuel to keep it going.

THE SIX IMPORTANT STEPS TO SUCCESS

When you start in real estate, most principals will talk about the market, getting stock and making sales. So the focus of all new sales people will be to get listings and sell them which is the final result. But there are six very important steps to take beforehand that are covered in the following chapters:

1. Goals
2. Planning
3. Prospecting
4. Presenting
5. Listing
6. Selling

Goals

You will never get anywhere in life without goals. They can be financial or personal and they are usually linked. Goals give you purpose and a way to measure your success as the journey begins on the way to a successful career. If you don't have any goals you are just a motivated idiot who lacks direction or focus. If you share your goals with others you are able to build a career with their support. Throughout my career as a sales manager, I love dealing with sales people who are goal-driven. I find them easier to work with and much more motivated when it comes to challenging times because they have something to aim for, not just something I want them to do.

Planning

Planning is building steps for you to follow – much like a street map – so you can see where you are going and plan how to arrive at your destination rather than wonder how to get there or just hope that you will. Your plan will be based on your goals and may include budgets, training needs and a timetable. Planning is a very, very important process and the next steps should not be undertaken until your goals and planning have become very clear and easy to understand.

Part of your plan will involve setting benchmarks for performance and ensuring you stay accountable along the way. You won't get every part of your plan perfectly right because things will pop up which you didn't expect or maybe you didn't have enough knowledge, but remember it is all about learning. Planning enables you to correct yourself when you veer off in the wrong direction and your goals seem to be getting further away rather than closer. Very much like sport, you need to start with some sort of game plan and be your own coach and adjust your plan as the game unfolds. When you first start devising your plan you will need to fine tune it quite a bit. This is part of the fun of learning although sometimes you may not like the lessons you learn. Just as you did with your goals, share your plan with the people who can help and encourage you, such as your sales manager, mentors or family.

Prospecting

Prospecting is the step that needs to involve a system that continually produces opportunities for you. It may become repetitious but the more systemised the better as this is one of the steps sales people let go of. When they do, they lose momentum and then have to start all over again. Prospecting is about regularly generating appointments that are qualified to ensure success when you make your presentation or show a property. Following scripts and dialogue training are very important as is a good understanding of how databases work. These are all the right tools to be able to prospect well.

For many, prospecting is a huge challenge due the amount of rejection you receive but, once again, fine tuning will help and in time you will get it right. Then it will become automatic and start to feel easier. Never stop prospecting because it takes time to get started and once you stop it is harder to get going again. You need to find a way to enjoy prospecting so maybe replace the word 'prospecting' with the word 'hunting'. Make it fun where you can. Mix it up so you don't get bored and stop doing it through lack of interest. The danger in prospecting is when you feel it is flowing and then you forget to keep filling up the funnel. Always be careful you have things in the pipeline for the future as well as today.

Presenting

Presenting is the main show time experience of real estate. This is where you need to be able to influence people to trust you. They need to believe that you are the agent who will get the best result and represent their best interests at all times. This is where you have to be very flexible and have sensational scripts and dialogues prepared. You also need a huge belief in yourself, as well as the brand you represent. People are looking for someone they trust and who will listen to their needs. Some refer to this as completing an appraisal, for me an appraisal is where you tell someone a value. Presentation, rather, is about showing interest in the clients' goals and letting them know how you are going to help them achieve their goals with the help of you and your services.

Listing

Listing is the service and the work involved in getting the property into the marketplace. Listing strategies will have been selected in consultation with the owner and to be successful you need to ensure strong communication is kept up as things progress. You will need to coordinate the processes and systems you use to get the best results for your client when marketing their property. 'Listing' is the term I use in the six steps to mean getting the property ready from an agency's point of view; to deliver the service you need to and to make things happen. This all comes together only after the owner picks you to help with their goals and you put the structure together to attract the best interest in their property. You can't do that without their permission in writing to do so and this is what listing is all about.

Selling

Selling involves negotiation and also reviewing the market place. The marketing plan has to be followed to make sure you are progressing and if not the strategies may need to be changed as well as the price if necessary. Naturally, selling has a lot to do with negotiating the final contract and any conditions. You have to handle the contract through the whole process to ensure that by the end of the experience all parties feel fairly treated and will sell with you again in the future. Selling is the final result but you also need to ensure the property is 'sellable' as well. Selling is about far more than just the dollar amount you achieve at the end of the process. Although closing the deal is of course a very important step.

Six Steps to Success Matrix

Goals → **Planning** → **Prospecting**

Goals	Planning	Prospecting
• What are your dreams? • Short term? • Medium term? • Long term? • Personal? • Business? • **Be clear!**	• How? Why? When? What? • Get organised! • Create a measure system that keeps you focused. • Create balance. • Work out what success equals. • Do your numbers. • **Minimum performance levels**	• Quality questions = quality results. • How many people do you speak with? • Are you talking to the right people? • How do you find them? • Use your marketing machine. • **Scripts and dialogues** • **Minimum performance levels**

Selling ← **Listing** ← **Presenting**

Selling	Listing	Presenting
• Create huge buyer database – how many names do you need to hold? • Negotiate from strengths. • Use technology – e.g. a good database. • How many buyer appointments do you need a week? • How do you handle buyer enquiry. • **Minimum performance levels**	• What are your targets? • Create a plan and system that works. • Service clients well and business grows. • **Minimum performance levels**	• Got to get in front of people who are selling. • Value proposition. • What conversion rate do you need? • **Scripts and dialogues**

"Your belief creates your energy"

Above is the Six Steps to Success matrix. We will go into each of these steps more deeply throughout the book. As you go along during your career, when things are not firing, one of these elements may not be working for you. Make sure your goals are clear, then your vision going forward will be too. Most agents focus on the last three steps when in fact the real power to make things happen is in the first three.

2. STEP ONE – GOALS

The journey starts with the first step and that step is to understand why you are in real estate and what you truly want to achieve. In other words, what is your main goal? Goal-setting is very, very important – so important that it comes first in my six steps to real estate sales success. You need to focus to succeed and to have something to focus on all the time.

The definition of a goal is:

"A goal is a dream with a deadline"

I have been a goal-setter almost all of my adult life. Goals are like maps, they show you where to go and how to get there. They also need to have a timeframe – a deadline – or as the definition infers, they are little more than a dream.

To activate others you must activate yourself first and to do that you need a purpose for your day. You need to internalise your goals and that will in turn guide you in the right direction because of your focus. I personally had a time in my life when I stopped goal-setting and it was the worst time of my life. I would lie in bed and not bother getting up because there was nothing to get up for. I had no focus, nothing to get me activated.

Beware, even with a map, sometimes you get lost when you turn down the wrong street. Don't worry if this happens, just learn not to go down there again. The aim of this book is help create a map (plan) that leads to the fastest route to success in real estate for you.

SETTING YOUR GOALS

My advice to you is to draw up a list of goals that you'd like to achieve in the next three, six, nine, and twelve months. Then look further ahead to the next three years. Do this for both your business and personal life. Do it now. I've made it easy for you – just jot your goals down in the spaces provided below.

My three-month goal is:

Business: _____

Personal: _____

My six-month goal is:

Business: _____

Personal: _____

My nine-month goal is:

Business: _____

Personal: _____

My 12-month goal is:

Business: _____

Personal: _____

My three-year goal is:

Business: _____

Personal: _____

Did you do it? Now use the space above to write down next to each goal notes on how you are going to achieve it. List the costs involved or sacrifices you need to make and the ghosts (bad habits) you need to get rid of to be successful.

REWARD YOURSELF

Of course it's not enough to just set and forget, you need to have an accountability system. This means reviewing and measuring your progress. Very importantly, ensure you reward yourself when you achieve a goal. In your own mind, be aware of the positive things these goals will bring to your work life and your family and also be aware of the consequences of your failure. Stop and measure regularly and adjust your actions when necessary.

It may sound complex but it is only complex when you don't do it.

Share your goals with people you need support from and identify whose help you will require to make these things happen.

SEEKING SUPPORT FROM YOUR COLLEAGUES

If you are already in an agency that is positive and supportive then you are off to a great start. The culture around you is very important to help you grow, however be clear that not only do you need to work with a group of nice people but this group needs to be driven and goal-focused too or they will just slow you down. Be with people who will test you and who are focused as well. A competitive office by nature is a good thing. It will encourage you to improve.

Ensure you are in an office where the boss is a decision-maker. You need to be with a good leader to achieve your goals, otherwise you will become frustrated and that will limit your ability to succeed.

When you start out in real estate you need to ensure you receive regular training at least once a fortnight. If you cannot find that within the office then find it externally. Add it to your list of short-term goals – to embrace training and personal development opportunities.

A systemised office is excellent for support. Accept that other people within the office have more experience than you and soak up as much of it as you can. Find out who the top people are and have a coffee with them. Don't be surprised if the answer to their success seems simple. Simple is beautiful. Life is not complicated, only people are.

Remember, you will not be able to change a culture to match your goals. Offices have their own feel and that is greatly determined by the leader. You will have little chance of changing them. So if your current office is not aligned to your overall goals then you may have to consider making a move.

Although external support is vital, you are required to give back.

Be a strong team member yourself. You only get what you put in, so don't just be a taker.

PLANNING YOUR SUCCESS MAP

As I said before, you need a map (plan) to plot your journey to success. You need to find out what steps are required. Real estate is a numbers game; the more people you talk to or communicate with on a daily, weekly and monthly basis, the greater chance you have of success. So initially you need to set goals and a plan of action to make sure you meet and communicate with as many people as possible.

By doing this you will be designing a strategy which will develop your effective habits for creating business.

The question I ask you now is, if agent A speaks to two people a day and agent B speaks with 20 people a day, who do you think will have greater opportunities in the future? If you answered "agent B" then you are on the right track. Make this one of your goals: to talk to 'x' amount of people a day.

There are two main spheres from where you will generate business which we talk more about in the chapter on prospecting.

Include your personal connections in your plan

The first sphere is your personal database, that is, the people you already know. Many new to the industry say they don't like doing business with friends and relatives. Personally, a lot of my initial business was from my personal sphere of influence in my office in Midland (WA). My top sales person generates 80 per cent of her business from her personal database too.

The question I would ask you is, if you drove past your best mate's house or sister's house and they had one of your opposition's for sale signs out the front, how would you feel? The other thing I would mention is, it is only human nature that you will become friends with some of your clients. So don't tell me they will become people you don't deal with.

The only reason you should not deal with family or friends is if you truly believe you cannot be a good agent for them and that the opposition are all better than you. There are circumstances when it's best to leave something to others but at least pick up a referral fee from the other agent.

Include professional connections in your plan

The second main sphere of people who you need to include in your plan are the people you meet in the market. Examples include buyers at home opens, phone inquiries, office phone-ins, referrals from the rental department and so on.

Creating your plan

You need to create a plan of activities that is balanced and covers these main spheres effectively each week.

Your prospecting plan has to be non-negotiable and will create the habits of success. You need to generate appointments for yourself daily. When you start, the last place you can afford to be is standing around the office kitchen drinking coffee and chatting with the lowest performer in the office.

Set goals and establish a benchmark for all your activities, some numbers that you have to achieve day in, day out. The first six weeks of your career are crucial. They set the foundations to many of your habits of the future.

Before you start your career in real estate, talk to as many successful people in real estate as you can, as well as successful people in any other business you know.

Don't be shy about telling people you are going into real estate, tell everyone. There is nothing worse than when you bump into an old buddy and they say they didn't know you were in real estate and if they had they would have given you their house to sell.

I have told every sales person who has ever started with me to make a list of everyone they know, even if it's from 20 years ago, and send them an email when they start. They are often surprised by how much business this generates. Then, you always need to keep in contact – whether it is by email or in person, just don't forget to do it!

YOUR BOSS WILL SET YOU GOALS TOO

As well as setting your own goals, your boss will have goals – targets – for you to work towards. Make an appointment with your future boss even before you start and ask them about your targets. What do they expect from you? Find out about all your meeting structures and if you will have a farm area (we will discuss farm areas later on). Then when you have begun your new job, ensure you catch up with your boss once a week for discussions once you start.

LAYING THE BEST FOUNDATIONS

Your main goal should be to create a plan that stops you from becoming the best kept secret in real estate. You need to plant this thought in your mind: *"You are the best agent you know"* – otherwise you'd better recommend someone else.

Ensure you are balanced from the beginning. By having a plan, you will create balance for yourself and an effective way of measuring your performance. The foundations to any building are very important and so should be the foundations to your career. Your initial habits need to be strong and focused otherwise you will be spending many hours later trying to undo those poor habits you have developed.

You will notice that many agents only take on agents who are new to the industry. The main reason for this is they are more trainable than experienced sales people and they haven't developed bad habits which need to be undone.

TRADITION IS NOT ALWAYS THE BEST WAY

Real estate is changing all the time and you need to understand that. What people were doing three years ago may not be relevant to today's market conditions. This next story illustrates this point perfectly.

At the Smiths, all the generations gather together each year for Christmas and they enjoy their ham which has been prepared the same way for as long as anyone can remember. Sarah, the youngest in the family, is busy learning from her mother the traditional way of preparing the ham. Sarah notices that her mother cuts both ends of the ham off before placing the ham in the oven for cooking. She asks her mother why she does this.

"I don't know, Nanna showed me this so best you ask her".

Sarah then goes to her nanna and asks the same question, why did her mother cut the ends off the ham? Nanna replies:

"She would have seen me do it and I was shown by my mother to do this. But to be honest, I don't know why we do it, best you ask your great-grandma".

Off Sarah runs and she asks her great-grandma, "Why did you cut off the ends off the ham when you cooked it?" Great-Grandma replied:

"I did it because the ham wouldn't fit into the baking dish if I didn't cut the ends off".

When you start with a company and you are being shown how things are done, be wary that you are just not cutting off the ends of the ham because other people did before you. Ask yourself why am I doing this? Is this the most effective and simple way to do this? It may just be time to develop your own systems.

TIME MANAGEMENT

Of course you'll never achieve your goals if you don't have time! Time management is a very important skill. We all have the same amount of time yet some appear to achieve more than others.

In real estate, it is essential for you to have good time-management skills. No one is perfect at this science but there are many ways you can help yourself to manage your time better.

Using a diary is a good start and using it effectively is the key. Don't try and be everything to everyone. Focus on what you can do and leave the miracles to the others. Having the ability to focus on tasks is the first step. Compiling a to-do list helps you to fine-tune your focus.

Set yourself daily goals on your to-do list. Each day you should have a list of minimum objectives that include a balance of prospecting, servicing owners, showing properties and presentation appointments. All are very important tasks so a balance is required.

Time spent within the office should be focused to assist in the basic tasks, nothing else. Delegation is an effective way of ensuring you focus on the dollar-productive activities in your day. Many high-performers, particularly on the east coast of Australia, have personal assistants who do the non-dollar-productive work. There is no use being a great presenter if you never attend any presentations due the fact that you are a poor time manager. If your paperwork takes you forever, you are losing time that could be spent prospecting or you could be creating appointments for yourself to present.

As you go through the day ask yourself "is what I am doing in line with the goals for the day?" If not, stop and do the things that are.

Sometimes you won't achieve all of your daily goals so they must be reallocated to the next day or a timeframe later. If you have done your bit for the day, go home and relax and be with the family – don't be at the office because that feels like the right thing to do.

Handle paperwork only once wherever possible. Many agents become hoarders of pieces of paper and then all day they are shuffling them around. Every office has one (a hoarder). I bet you have seen them before.

Qualifying people you meet is an excellent way to save valuable time. Time is the most valuable thing we have so don't waste it for any reason.

Your ability to set goals and establish healthy work habits has an enormous bearing on your time management. Routine can save time, providing it is a good routine; a bad routine is destructive to your career. An easy way to have a balanced routine for the future is to construct a weekly planner of main events that happen every week, such as your meetings in the office and with clients. You may ring your vendors (owners) every Monday at ten o'clock – that should be pre-booked in your weekly calendar so that it is done and not forgotten.

Other important habits should be scheduled into your week including time for family and for keeping fit. Also, it's a good idea not to fill the week completely but to keep some time free for unexpected appointments that could lead to new business.

There are many books on time management you could read to keep motivated to manage your time the best you can. Time management is about taking control of your life rather than wasting it and I know which I personally would prefer to do.

Time management in many ways is about energy management. You can't do things when you are tired and there is no sense having time to spare if you have no energy to take advantage of it and enjoy it. Balance is important in all areas of your life as we have already mentioned.

Don't get caught up with time-wasters. This is a common problem for agents who think they have to listen to people who are wasting their time. Yes, have manners, but also respect your time and place a value on it. If others aren't respecting your time move on, you can't afford to waste your life on drop-kicks. Manners are one thing, wasting your valuable time is another. You need to draw the line at times, that is simply part of life and business.

Now you have set your daily, weekly and long-term goals let's move onto the next step on the road to success – planning.

3. STEP TWO – PLANNING

The second step on the journey to real estate success is an extension of the first goal-setting step. Both are part of the preliminary work you should do at the beginning of your career in sales.

The main reason for a plan is to create the right success habits on a regular basis. You will already have bad or unproductive habits whether you have been in real estate for one minute or 20 years. Everything you do daily is a result of your habits from the past. For example, if you are a person who is always late, that habit does not occur over night and will take time to change.

WHAT DOES A GOOD PLAN HAVE IN IT?

A good plan will include a variety of activities to generate appointments that will keep you in touch with your different spheres of influence. You will need to have block-out times for various activities and they need to be 'not negotiable', meaning they will be completed *no matter what!* A plan is about accountability, not to others but to yourself. It is a measuring stick for you to use on an ongoing basis.

A plan is like a street directory or a map. If you were asked to go to a street in a suburb you have never heard of before, the first thing you would do is refer to a map to find out how to get there. As you progress towards your destination in your car, you would have that map next to you to refer to in case you turned down the wrong street and also to ensure you were heading in the right direction.

Your plan is exactly that, a map with directions for getting you to your destination. If you can master this you will not only be successful in real estate but it could also have a major influence in all aspects of your life. The old saying "Those who fail to plan, plan to fail" is so true and this is something that cannot be over-emphasised.

Many people fill their diaries with random appointments not with activities that guide them to success. Then at the end of the week, they state how busy they were. Instead, you should be able to measure how successful you were each day and each week. There has to be measurement and control in your day, a balance between activities and appointments.

When you first start in a new real estate sales role, the initial learning curve is steep. The information you have to take in initially will appear daunting.

It's a good idea to start planning in bite-size chunks. Plan activities for a 14-day or 30-day period. Your plan needs to have a number of set appointments to cover both your business-generating activities with your network, as well as having time for your training and, more importantly, maintaining your balance outside of work. You would have already noticed I use the word balance regularly. Your partner, wife or husband and family must be part of your plan because your life outside of real estate can have as much influence on your success as the people you work with.

Your plan is also a great test of your true desire to be successful. To establish a plan you have to be very clear in your goals and have a clear understanding of what steps need to be taken, that is, what a plan is based upon.

Why only a 30-day plan? What about long-term planning?

Your long-term success will be the result of a number of plans that you have created, that all feed up into each other. Very few people write down their goals and even fewer write down what steps need to be taken. This in itself will give you an advantage.

Be realistic in the beginning. Your initial plans will need work but the point is you have something to measure against not just 'guessology' which is how most of your opposition will be operating.

You must have a 'stop and measure' mentality when it comes to knowing which direction to go in. You need to devise some way of assessing what you have done and a way to identify your strengths as well as your weaknesses. Remember the map example, when you follow a map (your plan) you have a clear way of knowing where you have come from and exactly where you need to go next.

I will share something with you about decision-making. I ask this question regularly to my staff as well as to myself: "Is what I am doing in line with what I need to do to get to my objective?" If the answer is no, then let it go.

I have sat with hundreds of agents all over Australia and discussed planning with them. They all agree it is the only way to go, but too few will take up the challenge. For you, this is the best news you will ever hear. Will you take advantage of this or simply be like all the others? The choice is yours!

MAKING A PLAN

Your challenge is to bridge the gap, which exists between where you are now and the goals you intend to reach. Developing a plan is actually laying out the structure of events that have to occur for you to achieve each goal.

Divide your plan into a sequence of easy-to-do steps.

If you fail to reach your goal, divide again.

I have created a matrix for a basic plan for your work. I have given an example of a basic plan for a sales person overleaf so that you have a guide to work from.

You don't have to fill in all the boxes. You can move them around but always maintain the minimum of what you believe needs to be done to create and support your goals. Review this planner with your manager regularly and don't be scared to try new things, but don't over-complicate your planner. It should be a simple document of what you are aiming to achieve, and it's best to work through it with a sales manager or coach in the early days.

You will have decided your income goals and listing goals, etc. when you created your business plan. Review these also and note them down in the table overleaf.

WEEKLY PLANNER

Time	Monday	Tuesday	Wednesday	Thursday	Friday	Saturday	Sunday
8-9	Follow up	Advertising	Buyer management	Training	Weekend reminders		
9-10	Update data	Sales meeting	Data review	Follow up past prospects	Checklists for weekend	Sarah's netball	
10-11	Feedback to owners	Review your stock	Follow up hot sellers	People I know calls	Follow up hot buyers		
11-12							
1-2		Door knock					
2-3		Door knock					
3-4						Matt's footy	Opens
4-5	Prospecting – phone						Opens
5-6	Prospecting – phone						Opens
	Prospecting – phone					Opens	

Income goals:

Weekly: _____

Monthly: _____

Annual: _____

Listing goals:

Weekly: _____

Monthly: _____

Annual: _____

Sales goals:

Weekly: _____

Monthly: _____

Annual: _____

Presentation goals:

Weekly: _____

Monthly: _____

Annual: _____

YOUR FIRST WEEK

If you could just take the energy that you have in your first week and inject yourself with that energy a year later and every year after that, you would be a super-agent. You start out so keen – if a little nervous – but without restrictions and the world of real estate is an exciting adventure.

Unfortunately in the first week you develop some of your worst habits. These include *not* qualifying buyers and *not* working to a plan or spending time developing a plan. Many come into this industry and within a week they are out there on their own and they lose the habit of regular training because they are too busy doing anything rather than learning the right ways or better ways of doing things.

Develop a habit of talking with the best agents around you to find out their success habits – do this straight away not later when you're frustrated. If you get a chance to shadow a top performer, take it. Attend appraisals with him or her, call into some home opens (open for inspections) of your opposition before they know who you are. Learn how they deal with the public and do it better.

Develop a base marketing strategy and work out how much these efforts will cost. Then sticking to your budget create a program to follow. This template overleaf may help you. Use the abbreviations below the table to develop your own marketing plan.

Develop the habit of doing script training a minimum of once a week (more about this later).

Start communicating. Ensure everyone you know receives a message from you, in the form of a letter or email, letting them know you are in real estate. Then follow up with regular communication at least every two months. Set up a base weekly planner and revisit weekly for the first three months and fine tune it. Maybe create a points system for yourself so you can measure your activities. Set yourself a benchmark of meeting no less than ten people a day and give them your business card. Start building new relationships and re-establishing old ones.

Set up the rules with your principal around what he or she wants from you and understand how they will assist you. What are the minimum performance levels they expect of you? Your head

ANNUAL PERSONAL MARKETING PLANNER

	Jan	Feb	Mar	Apr	May	Jun	Jul	Aug	Sep	Oct	Nov	Dec
Week 1												
2												
3												
4												
5												

Telemarketing (TM)
Local Paper Marketing (LPM)
Newsletters (NL)
Local Sign (LS)
Editorials (AT)

Main Paper Marketing (MPM)
Mail out To Farm (MTF)
Door Knocking (DK)
Community Marketing (CM)
Shopping Centre Promos (SCP)

Letter Box Drop (LBD)
Personal Printing Notes (PPN)
Past Client Calls (PCC)
Buyer Nights (BN)
Past Appraisals Letters (PAL)

will spin in the first week but keep calm and things will be fine. You can control even the first day. Much of real estate is common sense.

It is very important to ensure you don't waste time with 'has-been' sales people. Ask the boss who is best to talk to, don't just talk to those sitting around you. They may be the non-productive sales people. Don't get me wrong, they are probably nice people but will they be able to pay the bills? Talk to the winners if you want to win. Be excited and be passionate about being successful.

Set yourself five important targets in your first couple of days:

- Decide upon the number of people you are going to speak to daily
- Aim to create an appointment a day
- Spend at least one hour a week listening to scripts and dialogues
- Establish a minimum performance level the company is expecting of you in the first three months because what you focus on, you get
- Record your activities in your diary daily.

YOUR FIRST MONTH

At this stage you should have had a couple of appointments, hopefully a listing or two and a sale. If you have not achieved all of these, don't panic, real estate is a marathon not a sprint. You should now be able to go through your diary and see what you have done in the last month and see what you haven't done.

At the end of your first month it is very important to sit with your principal and discuss what you have done and seek feedback on what you can do better. Measuring your proactive activities is vital because you are starting to develop serious habits in regard to these activities.

If you continue to do the same as everyone else, and do so poorly, these poor production habits will set in concrete and will take a lot of work to remodel. Human beings are creatures of habit whether good or bad. It is simpler to adjust sooner rather than later because later it will be harder and in all probability it will not happen. Be very, very honest with yourself and set further review times, preferably weekly if not daily.

Spend at least two hours or half a day pulling apart what you have been doing. You will be amazed how this will benefit you. Do not try and be a perfectionist just learn and adjust. I have been in the industry for more than 20 years and I am still learning all the time. I have never got anything 100 per cent right, but I know that I continually improve and give my best effort at all times.

The habits you have at the end of the month will be made worse within a year and then almost impossible to change. So review them and make necessary adjustments.

YOUR FIRST YEAR

Fifty-two weeks or twelve months into your career will seem like the longest time in your life. Your first year in real estate is a steep learning curve but it can be very enjoyable. Many sales agents in their first year lose opportunities because they are still learning the trade. You need to examine what you have done, as you should every year. You will get plenty of advice from everyone and it will take time to work out what is the truth and what is useful to learn from.

There is no reason you cannot be highly successful in your first year. The first year you need to focus heavily on creating your database to launch you forward in years to come. You need to benchmark against higher levels of people who you really know are successful, not just those you think might be.

During the first year there will be many temptations to get away from the basics and take shortcuts. There is no shortcut to success, there are only better ways.

The first year can be a shock for many, particularly if you have never been in a sales environment before. Ensure you have a balanced training schedule by listening to speakers on podcasts or CDs and watching as many training DVDs or videos as you can. Use your car as an educational vehicle by listening to CDs or podcasts while you drive to appointments or on your daily commute to the office. You are a captive audience when you are in the car.

Find a mentor to work with to keep you on track. Keep a dairy of what has and has not worked and fine-tune these areas later. Ensure you keep a score sheet of yourself annually – did you achieve your budget and the targets you had set for yourself to achieve in the first year? The best person to compete against is yourself, you can use the others as benchmarks.

TOOLS OF THE TRADE

Like any industry you need to have certain tools to be effective in what you do. The best laid plans will fail if you don't have the tools to do your job efficiently and effectively. I have listed below some of the things I believe you need.

- A reliable car that suits the market you operate in, with a good sound system to listen to training material or music for relaxation. It must be comfortable if you take clients out in it.

- Clothing that matches the market or the image you wish to portray to your clients.

- Training CDs or DVDs that you use regularly, or subscribe to online coaching or training. I have identified certain programs and coaches that I connect with best and I listen to them continually.

- A good software package (contact management system) for your database. You can either use the same system as your company or your own if the company does not have one. Very few agents do this effectively, if at all.

- A diary. Whether it be in physical format, on a computer, iPhone or iPad, whatever method best suits you for assisting in time management, use it.

- A business plan which should have measure points for you to refer to on a regular basis to monitor your progress and share with others to increase your accountability.

- A healthy attitude – what you feel inside you will display on the outside.

- A support group – that may be a coach, a strong sales manager/principal or simply a group of people who assist in keeping you on task and accountable.

- Basic systems to everything you do so that others can assist you when needed and it won't be difficult for them to learn them and achieve the same results for you – and even be open to their suggestions for fine tuning your systems.

- A smile costs nothing and can return a fortune. It is something you can't fake!

No doubt you will discover more, but this list will get you started or back on track.

4. STEP THREE – PROSPECTING

The word 'prospect' is defined by the Collins English Dictionary as: *"a probability or chance for future success, esp. as based on present work or aptitude".*

Prospecting is the make or break of real estate success. Many agents, when they first start in real estate, start really well. They prospect every day until one of two things happen.

The person either believes they are too busy to prospect because they now have listings or they simply get too caught up servicing the listings to maintain their prospecting activities. This is purely and simply an inability to manage time. Ignoring prospecting can soon become a habit because generally it is seen as a hard task and it's getting harder the more behind you get with it.

The second thing that can happen is ego. When success starts to flow, you forget it was disciplined prospecting that brought it and instead your ego takes the credit!

Prospecting needs be an automatic function if you are to succeed. As you start to create a cash flow and greater income, you can outsource some of your prospecting activities (for example phone canvassing, letterbox drops or anything you really believe that someone else could do better). It does not matter who generated the lead, it is about conversion. As you develop, you really want to focus on the 'specialist' things that you do that you can't and shouldn't delegate because these are what you do best.

There are many quality computer programs that generate follow-up material or cold canvassing campaigns for you. These will contact people you know through letters or email and send you simple reminder notes to contact them.

PROSPECTING IS THE ENGINE TO YOUR VEHICLE OF SUCCESS

Prospecting should not be looked at as something boring but as the main engine of your vehicle to success. Creating a network that works for you is vital and prospecting is the cornerstone to this.

I have met many quiet and unassuming sales people who do not appear that dynamic until you start examining their sales figures. The thing you discover is that these top people have recognised the importance of prospecting regularly and generally they have set systems in place to make sure it is happening day in, day out. Their ability to network is invaluable, in many cases it can be a simple process of not being afraid to introduce themselves at functions and events.

For me, personally, prospecting was equal in terms of enjoyment to negotiating. I just loved creating a new opportunity for the client and myself. Helping people is something I enjoy enormously and I always saw prospecting as me going out to help people achieve their goals. It may sound a little soppy but I got a buzz out of meeting new people and helping them. So I never saw it as a task. It actually just became pretty much what I liked to do every day. I guess in many ways that was why I was successful very early on in my career.

I remember in my eighth month in real estate I had a good month. I listed 11 properties and sold 13 properties in eight days. It was a pretty busy time I guess. I had no assistance. I did everything myself. I didn't have a personal assistant. One of the so-called experienced sales people came up to me and said, "Lucky little run you are having – beginners luck, young fella". My reply was pretty simple: "Colin, I'm not sure all the people I talk to everyday see it that way. All I know is the more people I talk to the luckier I seem to become".

Every day I had a clear target in my head that I needed to meet 20 people who would take my card and hopefully one day ring me when they needed me. When you do that, day after day, week after week, something has to happen. Momentum creates momentum. I have always been a great believer in that.

People will only ever be as keen as you are about your future and prospecting is about helping you in the future, not always right there and then.

Make prospecting fun. Enjoy it. By the way, smiling gets you a lot of business even if you don't know what you are doing. And I can tell you, in the early days, I didn't have a clue!

FARMING AREAS

In most agencies throughout Australia sales people are allocated a farm area. This is an area which you prospect on a regular basis, with activities such as newsletters, letterbox drops, door knocking and telemarketing. There are a number of advantages in doing this for both the company and yourself.

Having your own farm area gives you an area to focus your activities on; it also gives you an opportunity to learn property values in a given area. It is impossible to know values in all areas straight up, so to learn one and build from there is a logical way to go.

From a company point of view, the farm area may be new for the company to grow into. It may be on the edge of its current market place, so the principal will be keen to support you as you are further expanding his or her company.

You will remember earlier in the book I talked about two spheres of influence for your business – your personal and business areas of influence. Your farm area is in the latter category. You will need to design a plan to work your farm area, as well as keep up with your continual personal marketing.

There is nothing better than being known as the area specialist. There are some great agents who effectively farm their areas but they are rare. Agents have varying opinions on how a farm should be allocated and how many homes should be in the farm. In the area where my agency is, we have suburbs which have as few as 350 and as many as 5,000 houses. The farms for my staff have a minimum of 1,000 houses and state-housing homes are not included in those numbers because they are not prospects for the sales person.

We assess how many potential sales there are per year for that area, based on the average number of sales from the last three years. It is my belief that the percentage of total income of the sales person generated in their farm should be no less than 30 per cent of their annual income, hopefully as high as 50 per cent per year.

The idea of a farm is to work your way through the entire area via the various prospecting methods throughout the year so that you become recognised as *the* local agent, *the* person to see when it comes to real estate.

You need to design a way to contact every person within your area at least three to four times a year minimum. Newsletters are a great way to display your knowledge of the area because they can be full of local news and recent real estate information that readers will find interesting.

You need to know everything about your area including information about schools, sporting clubs, bus routes, doctors and the list goes on.

SET YOURSELF PROSPECTING TARGETS

Your target every month should be to get at least two appraisals a week in your area, ideally one a day. Your plan should be aimed at achieving these results consistently. Farming is an ongoing process, not something you do when you have nothing to do. There needs to be contact with people daily if possible.

Telemarketing is a great way of introducing yourself to people. The ideal way is to first write to a prospect, then follow up with a phone call a couple of days later. Remember though, if your letter or email states you will call them then you have to DO IT! Otherwise you're dead in the water – your credibility has been undermined and you are not regarded as reliable. When you do make this follow-up call, your prospect will be expecting your call, so it is not such a cold call.

Now I want to think about how many people you know and then how many people you keep in contact with on a regular basis. Most of you will say "I know heaps of people". That's great but my second question is, how many of them do you keep in regular contact with?

Most of us have an inner circle of people we keep in contact with on a frequent basis. We have a closer relationship with some of our contacts than others. The number varies but it's somewhere between 20 and 50.

Now imagine if you could tap into these inner circles (areas of influence) of the people in your farm area. You will receive business from them and from areas outside your farm area through referral business. I have had people in the past in my farm who I had never done a transaction for, but who had referred me to no less than ten people. This was because they simply believed I was good at what I did. When they decided finally to sell their property, I was in the forefront of their mind to get their business. Prior to this, they have been great advocates for me and will continue to be.

BUILD YOUR REFERRAL BASE

Your aim in your farm area is to create as many advocates as you can, as quickly as you can. Your first listing (property for sale) will give you great confidence and will help build your reputation within the area because when you get results for people, the chain results start to happen.

On the other side of the coin, if you stuff up, people will know that too. You have to have a very positive outlook on the area you are farming. Everyone you talk to may be connected in some way with that area and they want to hear about the positives. You never know who you are talking to. I can give you an example.

I did a presentation (appraisal) with a gentleman on a property in my farm area. During the discussion he had expressed that he felt the area which his home was in was not that interesting. He felt his property also wouldn't generate much interest because it wasn't a true character home which he thought people desired more in the area. I explained that the fact his home was more modern than many of the homes in his suburb was an advantage. There were many people who desired his location who wouldn't necessarily choose the older homes because normally they needed more upkeep.

Later that day I received a phone call from a lady who asked me to list her home for sale. I had not met her and had not seen her house at that stage. When I arrived to do the paperwork I was amazed how positive she was towards me. I then asked her how she got my name. She advised me that I had appraised the house of a good friend of hers earlier in the day and he recommended me as the agent to sell her home. He had told her that he had three other agents appraise his property earlier in the week and they had all been negative. I had the right attitude and that was why she felt I could help her. I sold her property within a week and later listed and sold the gentleman's home two weeks later. By the way, I had only been in real estate three months. It is amazing what a positive approach can do.

Farming areas is a great way to build a referral base in a short period of time, if done correctly. I had a husband-and-wife team work with me. They had been in real estate for a number of years and had done very well but they had never farmed before. To be part of my team you must prospect a farm area. They found it a challenge initially but later they were very grateful. They found their time management was stronger and their income went up and they enjoyed what they did more. At one stage they had a 60 per cent market share of sales in the area and people would ring them because they were the agents people had to have. Wouldn't you like that to be you? It can happen but it takes effort and patience.

Farming is about building a useful database to work from and build your future on. In our office, sales people have to demonstrate that they work their areas on a regular basis. All leads for a particular area are given to the area specialist (farmer) unless the clients request someone within the office they already know or have been referred to.

GENERATING APPOINTMENTS

Real estate is a numbers game; the more numbers you do, the greater the opportunity for you to succeed. We've covered farming but you should also be aiming to generate business opportunities in other areas as well.

As I explained, you have two major spheres of influence and you need to use both of these to generate appointments – especially early in your career. Unfortunately you are going to burn a few of the leads you generate so therefore to get a reasonable result you need to generate greater numbers. You won't have the referral business that experienced people have when you are starting out, so you need to stimulate regular appointments yourself. Referrals will come later – you need successes in the field first and you need to keep building your network.

DATABASE BUILDING

Building a database of contacts allows you to keep in touch with as many people as you can as often as you can. Your network of contacts needs to be tracked so that you know how effective they are. Different parts of your network are useful for different reasons.

People on your own personal contact list made up of family, friends and old colleagues from previous jobs need to be sent different communications than those you send to prospective buyers. So to effectively use your database you need to divide it into different categories, the most common being:

- Current listings
- Possible listings
- Past appraisals
- Buyers
- Past clients
- Business contacts
- Personal.

Be careful not to create too many categories. Keep it all as simple as possible.

Let's look at each category in turn.

Current listings

This category is self-explanatory for these are the properties you are currently marketing. You might like to set up a weekly system to report to these clients through email or mail. Many agents tend not to send a lot of communication to owners when they are marketing, but I think it's important to forward copies of articles that may be relevant to the client. Also, a regular marketing report displays you are on the ball and accountable. There are times when extra conditioning of an owner (particularly concerning realistic sales prices) is more effective.

Possible listings

I have often bumped into someone who has said they are thinking of selling and I have failed to diarise it; or worse, I haven't remembered to follow up with them. You should always do some form of follow-up to show you are keen. Also, sometimes people forget where you work or that you work in real estate. A follow-up email or letter system is as good as any but that choice is up to you.

Past appraisals

As a result of your appraisal, you will have an idea of when the owner wants to sell so you should construct a system that works in line with the owner's timeframe. If a person says they're not quite ready to sell but will be ready in two months' time, a combination of calls, letters and emails can be a very effective way to keep your name in the forefront of their mind. Never assume that people will get back to you.

Buyers, once qualified, are placed into a system which regularly reminds agents of their needs, making it possible for agents to call or forward relevant information to potential buyers. Some companies have cross-match systems which match buyers to new stock in their office or marketplace, and keep in touch with buyers through email. Some internet inquiries are linked to certain databases and the data is processed automatically, which is very handy and saves you time. However, this data is useless unless you use it.

Past clients can be an assortment of different people; from people you have sold houses for, people you have sold houses to and people you have completed business with in past occupations.

Anyone you have had a successful transaction with in the past should be on this list and should be forwarded information. Sending out a regular newsletter can help to keep you in their minds and this will hopefully generate referral business too. Sending anniversary cards to people who have bought from you can also be very effective.

Business contacts

This list includes other agents and property professionals who you may get on well with, such as settlement agents, finance brokers, tradespeople you have used for repairs on property and local businesses. Keep in contact with these people via newsletters, email or post.

Many companies have very effective systems; the only problem is the lack of support the staff gives in the form of input. I have not met anyone who can keep in contact with all of their database without using a computer. If your company doesn't have good software to manage your database for you, find some of your own and make it work.

With an effective database, your business will grow faster. You will have to trust me on this. Don't think that just because you may not like getting letters from people chasing you for business that you shouldn't send similar letters to your database. There are a lot of people who appreciate being remembered and reminded. There is only one way of increasing your income without increasing your efforts and that is database mining.

There are many agents who don't have effective databases. These are the agents who sell a home to someone then three years later that person sells through someone else. The main reason for this is it's not the client's job to keep in contact, it is yours. If you choose to forget them then they will forget you. Most completed transactions with clients are positive, so why would you not want to help them again sometime in the future? Don't forget about all the referral business you might miss out on by not keeping in touch.

A high percentage of people don't sell through the person they purchased through and the main reason, according to my research, is that they can't remember who they bought through.

The choice is yours.

Personal

Ensure you are in contact with your personal database on a regular basis too. Do it in bite-size chunks and ensure it is frequent. It doesn't have to be in person; keep in touch by email, newsletter or through association, e.g. people you have in common. This will keep you on their shopping list and keep them as advocates to generate business for you. You need to be pushing yourself out there all the time, don't wait for things to happen.

There are three types of people in this world:

- Those who make things happen
- Those who watch things happen
- Those who wonder what happened.

Which one of these are you?

PROACTIVE PROSPECTING PAYS OFF

Business will not just walk in and say "here I am". If it were that easy, anyone could do it. Sales people who can make things happen or generate appointments regularly are the top players in the game. We have talked about having a plan and this is a simple reminder that you have to have prospecting in your plan of action on an ongoing basis.

You need to be proactive, that is, to talk and communicate with people all the time: hold home opens (open for inspections), continue door-knocking, telemarketing and cold business calling (calling in on local businesses and introducing yourself).

Catching up with past clients from your previous employment is a very good idea, as is catching up with old mates from your footy days or netball club. Everyone knows someone who is either thinking of buying or selling real estate. Some days you will find plenty and other days you will struggle, but that's OK because sometimes the timing is wrong or you are simply talking to the wrong people.

Appointments also create appointments, don't ever forget that. You meet people when you are out and about. Never ever go out without your business cards – and take plenty of them. No principal will complain about a sales person who hands out lots of cards. Trust me, I can tell when sales people are down, they don't order new business cards because they are not giving them to people they meet. Never, never, never sit and wait. If you can't get an appointment over the phone, get off your backside and go out and find one.

To get sales, you need to have stock. To have stock, you need to do presentations. To do presentations, you need to be making appointments, and lots of them, because not every presentation leads to a listing. It may give you an opportunity for a later listing but you also need decisions to be made now. Buyer appointments are important. Between 30 to 50 per cent of the market has to sell a house before buying.

Remember, if you are unable to stimulate appointments at a minimum of one per day you will struggle. Two appointments per day is preferable or a minimum of ten per week. You need to have an appointment result every day to be successful.

5. STEP FOUR – PRESENTING

SERVICE, SERVICE, SERVICE

The best service is what people are looking for from a real estate agent and it's so often what they do not get. Many people are lazy in selecting their agent which may seem strange considering the person they entrust with the sale of their property will probably be helping them with one of the most important decisions a home-owner can make.

(One thing to note, just because a sales person works within a large franchise does not mean he or she has been well trained. Neither does it mean that particular office operates in the most up-to-date and effective fashion.)

There are many property sellers who have not dealt with a real estate agent before and they simply choose the nicest agent. Again, this does not automatically mean they offer the best service and ultimately the best sale price for their home.

Agents need to develop a reputation for service and their company has to be known for its values.

Have you personally had an agent sell your property? Think back on that experience. Was it a good one? Or perhaps it was a bad one? Analyse the procedure you went though. Try to remember how it felt – the positives and the negatives. Did you feel part of the transaction or did you feel like an outsider?

Use your personal experiences as a vendor to create a benchmark to monitor your own performance. When you are starting out, you will have a lot of things to learn but always keep in mind how the end-user feels.

In your career, you will interact with the following main categories of clients/customers that an agency has – sellers, buyers, landlords and tenants. After meeting you, each of these people should feel that they have dealt with a person who will look after them to the best of their ability. Develop a reputation of being the person who makes things happen and keeps their promises.

Many agents fail to get back to people. This is not what you want. You would like repeat business and referrals from every vendor. So don't make promises you can't keep or don't have the authority to make.

IT'S NOT JUST ABOUT THE SALE

Never focus on the sale alone. Remember you are dealing with human beings who have emotions and want to be treated in a fair and reasonable manner. We are in a society which is moving faster and faster. Despite this, it is important you understand the service levels that people expect from you and that you can deliver them. Also keep in mind the demands of the individual, if they are too high you might have to walk away.

Why? You might ask. The answer is that if you take on business that you can't deliver, you could be doing more damage than good. There are a few people out there who you will never please.

This comes back to qualifying your prospects (which will be discussed later) but for now just be aware of qualifying. In your early days in the industry you will make mistakes and that is part of the learning experience. Keep in mind even the veterans make mistakes but it is what you do with those experiences that makes all the difference. In general, people are forgiving, providing you are being honest and they can see you are giving your best.

When you start with an agency, ensure you understand the standards the agency is aiming for and that you are not in conflict with them. Don't make the mistake of making promises the agency can't meet. Enthusiasm is a great thing but controlled enthusiasm is the best thing and it is far more effective and productive in the long run. When you first start, it is very important you listen closely to the principal of your company and other senior people as they have already made a number of mistakes that they can share with you and help you avoid.

DOING THE PRESENTATION (APPRAISALS)

When you do presentations to prospective sellers you have to convey to them in an easy-to-understand way that you will deliver the services they are looking for. Over time, your understanding of clients' wants and needs will improve. I would suggest that you go through as many home opens (open for inspections) as you can to see how others deal with buyers and how well they represent the sellers. You will be in for some real surprises. Once you've done this, go to as many presentations and buyer appointments as you can with your sales manager or top sales people and watch and learn.

More commonly known as an 'appraisal', the presentation is where a home-owner asks an agent around to get an opinion of the possible worth of their home, to inquire about what your company does and what your fees are.

A presentation, in my view, is a job application or partnership-building relationship meeting. Hopefully it is when you connect with the potential client. You should be nervous when you attend a presentation because anything worth having is worth being nervous for. When you have never met a person before it can be daunting at times but remember, they have not met you before either so they will be somewhat nervous too. So respect that.

How you generate a presentation will determine how many other agents are also invited to view the owner's home. When you are proactive and have self-generated your presentation, it minimises the possibility of other agents being invited to present. On the other hand, if the owner (possible seller) calls your office to request a presentation, then there is a high probability that they called other agents too. The Yellow Pages and internet are full of them (other agents)!

Do your homework

Qualify the owner over the phone as much as you can before you arrive to present. Very importantly, find out how long they have been in the property and what possible changes they have made since being there. This will help your preparation no end. Find out as much about the property as you can. Do your research and ensure your comparative sales data is accurate. Also, find out about similar types of property that are on the market. If you can uncover the vendor's motivation to sell and their timeframes, then you will know exactly how much time to invest in this presentation.

If they are looking to buy locally and you have the resources, take information on possible properties that may be of interest to them. That may also be a great way to test their motivation and may also create a sale for you.

It is vital that you have done as much research as possible because the vendors will have researched also. They will be aware of recent sales in the area and similar properties that are on the market. You don't want to be seen to not know your stuff.

When you arrive to do your presentation, try to ensure all decision-makers are at home. Sometimes they won't be and you may need to reschedule to do a second presentation to the other owner. If all parties are available, then all signatories will be at hand to sign you up, thereby saving you time. A decision can be made there and then because all parties will be fully aware of what you can do for them.

Do a drive-by first

Do a drive-by of sales evidence. A drive-by allows you see the 'Sold' signs of other homes that have sold recently in the area and the 'For Sale' signs of those that are currently on the market. This will focus your mind and give you information you can share with the owner when you start talking. As mentioned earlier, chances are the vendors will already know this information but it means you will be able to deal with any questions about recent sales and the prices of current listings.

Be on time

When you arrive at the property, be on time. You will be amazed at how many agents lose listings at this point, especially if the owner prides themselves on always being on time.

Be well-presented

Ensure you are neatly dressed and groomed. Don't be surprised if they are checking you out through the window as you arrive. Hopefully your car is well presented and clean too. Don't leave your car in the driveway to leak oil – not a good way to impress people.

Try to be relaxed

It is natural to be nervous when you arrive at a presentation, but try to relax. A good suggestion is to listen to your favourite music and get in the right mood while you are driving to the appointment. I know of sales people who put on music that really gets the heart pumping so when they arrive they are ready to take on the world.

You need to relax when you're presenting. Enjoy it! It is one of the major keys to your success in the future. You must control the presentation and ensure the owner feels as though they aren't just part of the process but that they are at the centre of what is happening. We all like to feel important and owners are no different.

Carefully think about what you would want as an owner and deliver not only facts and figures but also deliver a feeling to them. Many owners just want to trust someone who they believe cares for them. As an agent, you have to care but in a professional and a results-oriented manner.

Avoid real-estate speak

Your presentation has to be factual and interesting so use terms the vendors understand. Avoid jargon as much as possible – the owners may not admit it but they won't understand you. You need to have basic rules that keep you on track and ensure you are delivering properly each and every time. Do not be robotic. Be flexible, but also follow your hard and fast, basic rules to ensure predictable outcomes.

Personally, I believe it is always best to get the owners to talk to you. Open the conversation and allow them in as soon as you can, but if they talk too much, you have to have a way to control that as well. Getting the price right on the value of the property is only part of your job; a very small part of it. Building the relationship with the owners is your main focus and that is not buying a friend. It is about entering into a business partnership with these people and in time hopefully a long-term referral relationship.

Should you use visuals in your presentation?

Visuals are great to have with you at a presentation but ensure they are of the highest quality. You need to have a presentation that appeals to all the senses, or to as many as you can. Visuals and testimonials can be very powerful.

Many agents forward information to owners before they arrive at the appointment. These can help to pre-sell themselves and the services of the agency. They may prompt some great qualifying questions that will be asked as a result of what they have already read.

First impressions count

When you arrive at the house, you only have seconds before the owner will start making decisions about you. A smile is worth a million dollars. If you fumble in the greeting, you will lose control of your presentation very early. Eye-to-eye contact is very important with the client during a presentation and can never be underestimated.

Be positive in your approach and perhaps at the initial greet, thank them for having you over. Then set out how the presentation or meeting will go. For many this will be their first time, others may not have done this for a considerable time. From the second you walk in it is about relationship-building but remember the meter is running. Time is money and you must ensure you are not wasting their time or yours.

The vendors may have received advice or have their own preconceived ideas about what to look for in an agent. So don't be afraid to ask them during your presentation what they are looking for. If they have sold before, ask how that experience went and what they enjoyed and didn't enjoy about it.

Most of us do not enjoy interviewing people and therefore are poor at it. Owners are no different. You need to develop effective questions that determine their motivation, timeframes and desired final result. This will not happen overnight but with continual practice in role-plays or discussions with your peers you will become better.

What's your USP?

Quite often owners will pick an agent purely on how nice someone is because they have seen nothing that really stands out in many industries. It is said that they have not been presented with a 'Unique Selling Proposition' (USP).

You need to find something that makes you and your company stand out. It might be your website. It could be that the company has been the number one agent in the area for 20 years. It could be because you are the biggest or the smallest. There has to be something that will create an interest in the vendor in what you do and how that will benefit them. Why? Because they are looking to benefit themselves, not you. They are the most important person in their world.

SCRIPTS AND DIALOGUES

How you respond to questions presented to you will have a big bearing on your ability to generate business. Over time, you will hear many questions, but eventually you will discover that there will be continual repetition of the same questions and so it is very important to learn basic answers to these questions. It's also important not to sound rehearsed or shallow in your replies.

You must have a solid understanding of your answers. The reason for this is your response may lead to further questions, which may lead to a sequence of questions which, in turn, could lead into a positive result for you and your client. At times you may need to lead a client in a certain direction, through a line of questions and replies, which will give the response you need to close a deal.

Letting the other vendors feel they are being heard and are able to have a say is very important to them. People do not want to feel dominated, if they do they will respond negatively. You will need to learn how to dig deep sometimes to find out more and, at other times, you need to learn to simply shut up and listen.

Role-playing with other staff is a great way to learn. Many people don't like role-plays, but I personally prefer to make a mistake in front of a colleague rather than a potential client. When you make a mistake in front of your team mate it might cost you a little embarrassment, but in front of a client it may be worth tens of thousands of dollars. How many clients do you want to burn before you get it right? There are many quality scripts, training CDs and DVDs out there so invest regularly in these.

Go out with your top people in the office on presentations if you can, but practise and practise. Have the CDs playing in the car; use your car as a training venue. You will be surprised at what you will absorb. There are new challenges every day. By having confidence in what you say, business will become easier.

I suggest you practise your scripts and dialogues regularly; after all, how many poor presentations do you want to do before you get it right? It's an expensive way to learn.

If you are new in the industry, as well as going out with senior people, have them come along to your presentations with you. Ask them to point out things you missed or could have done better. Even if you have been in the industry for a while, get someone to come along every now and then. You may have developed bad habits that need to be fine-tuned. If you develop outstanding presentation skills your income levels will reflect this and be high.

Top presenters win the business – listings – and this is a skill you have to perfect. You will develop your own style in time. If you have sold your own property in the past, look back at what you thought the agents did well or poorly in their presentation to you.

You need to be flexible in your presentations because no two people are the same or have the same needs and wants. Be a great listener but also have powerful questions that will help you to build a relationship with the vendor and close the business. Observe as many different presentations as you can and build your own from there. It is a skill you have to master quickly and effectively.

If you miss out on a listing, don't be afraid to ring people back and ask them what you could have done better. Their feedback will be invaluable. It will ensure you don't make the same mistakes in the future.

As previously mentioned, role-playing is a great thing to do with your peers. You will receive feedback that will be powerful in the future – practice makes perfect. This is the part of your real estate training you will always be working on. No matter how long you are in the industry, markets change. There is always a question you have never heard before, which some maniac has told people to ask in some book by someone who claims to be the latest real estate guru!

HOW LONG SHOULD A PRESENTATION TAKE?

Last but not least, what is the ideal length of a presentation? How long should a presentation take? The answer will depend on how qualified the lead is before you arrive and how well you present. I know of agents who can do it in less than an hour and others who prefer to take longer. To ensure all points are covered you will learn as you develop but it will also be dependent on how the appointment was generated. Some people have decided on you because their friend said you were the best in the business. That is the type of appointment we all want.

Develop a system with flexibility, do regular training, do your homework on the area and have some fun. The rest will take care of itself.

6. STEP FIVE – LISTING

You've completed your presentation and you've won the business. Congratulations! You have now listed your first property. Listing is the fifth of the six steps on the journey to real estate success – only one step away from your first sale.

HOW DO I MAKE MONEY IN REAL ESTATE?

It is the 'listers' who make all the money in real estate – it is as simple as that. Buyers ring the agents who have the 'For Sale' signs up. The listing agents are those who control the market. The public see the sold stickers on the listing agent's sign, not the selling agent's sign, unless they are also the listing agent. Listing agents make the world go round. They are the people who bring the stock to the market for buyers to see, they create the marketing for the inquiry.

There are agents out there who only do listing appointments, their buyer appointments are handled by their personal assistant who do the follow-up work on the buyer inquiries. Once you have become a strong lister things begin to accelerate. You still have to do the basics but when you have the ability to convince people to sell their home with you, because you are the best agent for them, your career will take an enormous turn in the right direction.

HOW DO I BECOME A GREAT LISTER?

The answer is simple: be a person with an action plan who generates appointments on a regular basis and builds their database regularly. Know your scripts and dialogues, deliver great service, have a positive nature and have an inner strength that drives you to be the best you can be, as often as you can.

Your presentations should leave the owner feeling like you are the only agent who can get them the best result – engage the owner and success will follow. That would be a great start. You will build your strength in your presentations with time and practice, but by training solidly with others in the office or with your manager you will move forward more quickly. Having confidence in yourself and your agency will always come through when presenting and will attract business in the form of referrals as well.

Qualifying prospects

Qualifying potential vendors is an essential skill you need to learn to be successful in real estate because you want to be spending the right amount of time on the right people. How do you qualify sellers? Well, you need to know the right questions to ask to save you time and effort.

Qualifying buyers is different again. When I first started in real estate, during my course at the institute, they made a big statement that 'buyers are liars'. At first that was my experience, but then I discovered that if I spent more time in the initial conversation qualifying the prospect I could save hours later. If the prospect does not have a reasonable idea of what they want, what chance have you got? You also need to probe deeply and find out as much as you can. You should then classify your prospect into one of four categories:

- **A** being 'red hot'. Someone who knows what they want and has a deadline that is achievable and within your expertise. They may also have a property they have to sell and are looking to do it now.

- **B** are owners who you know will list with you in the medium term – within the next 60 to 90 days. They may have a property to sell but you believe you can assist them in their search to find a property they would like to buy first.

- **C** is someone you contact and who may be in the early stages of the buying cycle. You tell them that if something pops up you will let them know and you will keep their name on the books to revisit later on.

- **NO WAY IN THE WORLD.** This final category comprises people who are simply dreamers and you don't have time for them no matter how nice they are. Time-wasters will cost you money and energy, and will burn you out.

Sometimes you will make the wrong decision about a prospect but you will make more right decisions than wrong. You need to develop questions that give you answers quickly and accurately, so work on a list of qualifying questions.

Timeframe is the big qualifier for both sellers and buyers. There has to be some form of urgency before they can be considered to be As. As and Bs are the people you really want to be dealing with – leave the rest for the other agents to fight over.

You have to remember you can't fit a square peg in a round hole. Here are two home truths:

- You will never be able to sell a house for an unrealistic seller who thinks his property is worth 50 per cent over the market value.

- You will never be able to sell a property to a person who doesn't know where they want to live and only wants to pay half the asking price.

Early in your career, you will be dependent on the opinion of your principal or sales manager for assistance in qualifying prospects. If necessary, seek their advice regularly on this subject because in the long run it will save you time and make you money.

We discussed scripts and dialogues earlier and these play an important role in this part of the real estate process. By having a good qualifying technique, your ability to close business will be very strong because you will be dealing with the right type of people.

CLOSING

What is closing? To me it is quite simply asking for the order. I have been to presentations where an agent has spent three hours with a person and still left without the business or a second appointment. Going back for a second appointment leaves the door ajar for another agent to come in and close the business that you failed to close.

Closing is determined by your ability to listen to what the client wants and knowing when to deliver the closing questions. Note I have said 'questions' (plural). Yes, sometimes you are lucky and it is one magical question that makes it happen. I can assure you now it will more often be the result of a number of questions you have asked and answered which has led to the final 'yes' by the client.

Many agents have trouble closing and therefore do poorly. Closing is something you can learn. Scripts and dialogues are a big part of learning to close. During a presentation you will come across many set-backs or objections. That is because people fear making the wrong decision. One good way to close is to tell people that although they may have fears, you will help to guide them.

I have stated earlier that you have to make appointments and then turn them into gold. The only way to do that is to close. You may have to try many different closes during the presentation until you get the right one. Or, as I said earlier, you have to build with a number of small closes that add up to one big one.

Here are some examples of closing questions:

- Mr Smith, when I take the photos of your property, is it better to do it in the morning or the afternoon?
- Did you want an advertisement in the newspaper this weekend? If so, we will need to get the text off tonight or first thing in the morning.
- Mrs Smith, if I arrange for the 'For Sale' sign to go next to the mailbox is that OK?
- When would you like me to start showing buyers through?
- How much notice do you need for inspections so that I can note that down?
- To get things going I just need you to authorise some paperwork, is that OK?

There are many CDs available to listen to as well as DVDs and videos you can watch on YouTube to help you practise closing. Role-playing with colleagues is a great way to practise your responses and the questions you need to use. After you have been in the industry for some time, you will discover that presentation questions are very similar. It is the response that is the key which determines your ability to close.

Many people want to be closed, it is not life-threatening. Closing takes practice and lots of it. The more you train and the more people you deal with, the better you become until you don't even realise you are doing it.

TIPS TO BECOME A GREAT LISTER

Top listers make the world go around in real estate, as we all now know. Top listers are great presenters who have practised and practised every part of a presentation over and over again. Many are very systematic in their approach, that is, they are in control of the appointment. I have met some who appear shy but they are really focused. Most are very competitive with other agents but more so with themselves.

They know their market well and have a confidence generated by their own success and knowledge. They don't make promises they can't keep, rather they under-promise and over-deliver. Here are some other attributes of great listers:

- Top listers have a very strong database, which they feed like a hungry beast.
- The top people have a presence when they walk into a room, an energy.
- They truly know what they are capable of and have no doubt in their mind they are the agent for the job.

- They know how to say no to bad business, e.g. over-priced listings and business they believe is not in line with what they believe to be good business.

- They are quick to qualify and back their judgment on that decision.

- They look for the positive in a situation not a negative.

- They have a record of successful sales and positive feedback from their clients, which they can demonstrate to a potential client.

- In many of their presentations they are not competing with other agents because the source of their lead is a referral they have generated by steadily building a relationship with this person over a period of time, using an effective system of contact.

Top listers do it and don't talk about it. They are champions in their field.

VENDOR MANAGEMENT

I have spoken with hundreds of vendors (sellers) over the years and the number one complaint from them is lack of communication. Many say that what is promised earlier in the presentation that encouraged them to list with the agent is rarely fully delivered.

Regular feedback is very, very important to the owner especially after an inspection by a potential buyer. There is no doubt in a seller's mind, particularly in the early weeks; they think everyone who walks into their home is going to want to buy their property.

A good agent will establish the rules early. If they don't, vendors will establish their own rules or seek the help of a friend who thinks they know everything an agent should know. They may have attended a course once so they know what should happen. Or their friend Ernie the expert, who simply has an opinion on everything, knows exactly what you should do to sell their property!

You need to be clear on what vendors should do when you are bringing someone around for a viewing. The most important rule here is that the vendors should not be there. Also, ensure you establish how – and when – you will communicate with the owners following an inspection so there are no unrealistic expectations.

Explain how you intend to present the property to the market – discuss the advertising or marketing plan and articulate why you have decided on this approach. With vendor management, you can never over-communicate but you can under-communicate. So be mindful of their expectations and have an understanding of how you will be dealing with the sale of their asset. Remember, the promises you made and then over-deliver and there should never be a problem.

COMMUNICATION

The majority of complaints about agents comes down to their lack of communication. It is not uncommon for a sales person to make promises and then not deliver. You're probably saying to yourself, "Hey that's not me. I always get back to people and do what I say I am going to do". If you are able to do that, then maybe you should write a book as well! The major issue is that many agents over-promise, lifting the client's expectations too high. As I've already said, it is better to under-promise and over-deliver.

It is funny that many believe they are good communicators and yet still have clients complain. It is very much about controlling the expectations of the client and keeping in line with the client's needs, not your own.

A relationship with anyone is built around communication – how you understand each other and what your expectations are of each other. Talking is only a part of communicating. In this day and age, with email and sms you can communicate in more time-efficient ways, and also with a trace. If a client questions your communication, you have the email or SMS trail to refer to and show them the information visually. Hopefully this leads to better understanding and also keeps all parties accountable, as well as giving you something to refer back to.

Verbal messages at times can be misinterpreted or twisted because we can't remember every word we hear or that we've said. The other thing with written communication is you have a greater control of time.

With face-to-face contact you communicate through body language as well as verbally. At times that can work against you.

The main thing clients want to know is what is happening with their property. Remember there is no doubt in their minds that their home will sell. If they don't hear from you they start to create their own rules on how a property should be marketed and they feel rejected by you because you are not paying attention to their needs.

Be careful about the promises you make and establish your rules for communication and stick to them. Under-promise, over-deliver and things will work out well for all parties and you will have a relationship for life rather than one sale.

7. STEP SIX – SELLING

Step six usually means you have your marketing in place and you're ready to show potential purchasers the property of their dreams! The best approach is via home opens.

HOME OPENS (OPEN FOR INSPECTIONS)

One of the most proactive steps an agent can take is to hold 'home opens' or 'open for inspections'. This is where the public can view the property and see you in action doing what you do best.

Many potential sellers visit home opens when they are shopping for their agent. You have the opportunity to present the property at its best which is how you want to present the property for the owner. The by-product of this is that a well-presented property makes you look better.

Your objective for the home open is to sell the property. The home open is ideal for the owners because they know when to go out, leaving you to show prospective buyers around. It is an organised event and it gives them a chance to work hard to present their home at its best for the potential buyers.

Home opens are also great lead-generator opportunities for agents because they get to meet buyers in the marketplace and they may get the chance to maybe list their home to sell as well. Buyers feel generally very comfortable at a home open. Many feel in control. It is the agent's job to qualify them and close if they're interested.

Home opens also create competition between buyers, particularly if they are seriously interested in the property and they sense that someone else may be interested too. This can at times make their offers better and their decision-making faster as they don't want to miss out.

Owners love home opens because it gives them a timetable to work to. They have a set deadline to make sure their home is presented at its best. Many agents in the industry call it 'show time' because they are on show with the home. Everything has to be at its best on the day. A well-organised home open can lead to some fantastic results.

You should ensure the home presents like a show home at the open for inspection. It is advisable for you to arrive early so you can inspect the home to ensure there is nothing to tidy up, such as towels left on floors to be picked up and put away, litter trays outside, etc. Also, ensure no valuables are left lying around.

It's a good idea to carry air-freshener in the car, just in case some homes have unpleasant odours, e.g. of stale tobacco smoke. You may want to open a few windows and air the house when you arrive prior to the open home.

At the home open, you need to ensure you have all your

marketing material at hand for the property you are presenting and information about you and the services you provide.

You have only one chance to make a first impression with the visitors to a home open so you have to make sure it is a good one. You need to have all the information on the home you are presenting. What chattels are included in the sale of the property? What is the zoning? Do you have a plan of the house?

Ensure you have a visitor's register and take the contact details of everyone who attends the open. You can then follow up for the owner later and maybe seek further feedback. Some agents have questionnaires that they give to visitors to give feedback to the owners on price and presentation.

QUALIFYING BUYERS

There is a range of visitors you will get at a home open:

- **Potential buyers** are who you want and the owner wants, naturally. This is why you have the open home, so qualify well by asking the right questions. Identify what bought them to the home open – the ad in the paper or on the internet? A drive-by? Each response will help you qualify each person.

- **Potential sellers** will visit home opens to get a feel for the market and to shop for their agent. They are in the investigating stage. Often they are also looking to buy and hopefully it is the house you are in.

- **Neighbours** will visit to give the owners feedback and many are like potential sellers, checking the market. Some are just sticky-beaks but they are often a good source of referral business to other potential sellers in the area.

- **Friends or family** of the seller. It is not unusual for someone in the family to attend to check you out to make sure you are doing your job. They also might be checking you out because the current owner has recommended you to them and they have come to see you in action.
- **Chronic lookers** are people who do exist but they are not common. They are dangerous time-wasters. You will see them in a variety of houses with differing price ranges – but they never part with their money. You will know them when you see them.

Each visitor should be approached in a professional manner. Qualify each visitor as they arrive. A simple question could be "Did you see the advert in the paper or on the internet?" Their answer will also give you an idea of how your marketing of the property is going.

TIPS FOR A SUCCESSFUL OPEN

I know many agents have music playing in the background at open homes, which I believe to be a great idea but be careful you select the music wisely. Remember, people are using all their senses when they inspect the home. I know of agents who ask owners to percolate coffee before a home open or have fresh cut flowers to help present the home better.

Beware the time-wasters who want to tie you up when you could be focusing on the real visitors in the property who have a true interest in buying. Always remember to follow through the promises you make to the people you meet. Have extra information on the area that the home is in, e.g. the local schools, public transport, churches, etc. These could be very important to the buyer.

Never use your phone while presenting a home. You cannot focus on a call and present at the same time. Always communicate with the owner as soon as possible about how things went. It's ideal to leave a note thanking them for how they left the home for you, with some short feedback. Then follow up later with a call that evening or the next day. Remember, they want to know straight away. They have put in the effort to present the property as well as they can and you need to respect that. Many relationships are affected by poor communication. This is the number one complaint made by the public about agents.

Always ensure that you give owners plenty of notice before a home open to allow them time to prepare, preferably a week in advance. Your 'Home Open' sign and 'For Sale' sign need to be positioned well, giving maximum exposure. Remember that they will be seen by potential future clients.

You need to have a system for your home opens which may include scripts and dialogues which you have practised when training in the office.

Your personal presentation needs to be at its highest level. This is also very much about your personal marketing as well, to ensure you are seen as a professional. Home opens are conducted throughout Australia and the public is very educated about them. So make them count for you and your owners. Create a great event rather than just go through the motions. When you enjoy your home opens, then you achieve better results.

I would recommend that you go through other agent's home opens where no one knows who you are. Then you can learn by observing what others do well and not so well. Look at the marketing your competitors do so you can build the perfect home open for you and your clients. Finding out what the others do can be very powerful. See what they are doing and do it better.

KNOW THE NUMBERS

In all forms of business it is important to understand the numbers. This is vital in sales. You need to analyse what numbers are required to be successful. You need to know how many homes are in your farm area and the number of properties that are owned by investors and owner/occupiers – so that you establish the right strategies for your marketing. This will take research and time. Initially this may seem daunting but once you have this information you only need to update your records which will take a minimum of effort.

Everything appears daunting in the beginning but in time once the structure is in place, the information you accumulate will make the biggest difference between you and your opposition. As mentioned throughout this book, to be successful you have to understand what you have achieved and learn from your failures and ensure you are in line with your goals.

Important ratios to know are:

- Number of appraisals (presentations) to listings
- Listings to sales.

You need to analyse your various marketing activities to ensure that the resources you are using achieve the right results to justify the cost involved. An example of this is letterbox dropping. You need to determine how often you should do it, how many mail pieces you should produce and who should do the mailbox drops.

You may discover over time that high gloss brochures have a higher response then black and white fliers. You may find that larger brochures work better than small ones. You may discover that telephone canvassing is more effective than direct mailing in certain parts of your area. You may also come to the conclusion that certain timeframes for phone canvassing are more effective than others.

In time, as your career evolves, you will discover that you may need to outsource certain activities. You can do this effectively once you understand the amount of resources required and the cost and likely results. You need to be able to invest your time not just use it. The numbers do not lie, they will tell you what does and doesn't work. Sometimes you will persist with an activity, not because it is effective, but because it is easier to do. These decisions are made on emotion rather than logic and with time management logic is far more important than emotion.

One of the main goals for all of us is around income so we also need to understand the numbers that make up your income. The important number is the potential income from your farm area and other spheres of influence. Other numbers you need to know are:

- Average sale price in the area
- Potential commission per sale in area (so you need to set a rate)
- Average sale time per property either in your area or your target.

These figures are the cornerstone to your income goals and they will help you to determine how many listings you may need to hold. The better your understanding of your numbers, the better your understanding of what the future needs to hold.

BENCHMARKING

Benchmarking your performance against some form of measurement is very important. You need to compare your results against another person's you aspire to be or against a target you may have set yourself.

Personally, in my career, I first set my benchmark against the top performer in the office. Upon achieving that, I then benchmark myself against my highest performance (similar to how athletes and sports people aim to beat their personal best, more commonly referred to as their PB). By doing this, great personal achievement can be felt.

Sometimes you don't need to be the top performer in your company to have a great income and enjoy your performance. Benchmarking is a good way to assist with your goals. It also gives you the opportunity to stretch yourself to new levels, which can be quite fulfilling. Be wary of how you are benchmarking yourself. Always ensure you are comparing yourself to improve your position not to justify it.

Benchmarking can be used also to assess your systems and timeframes, not just around your own personal sales performance. Adding comparisons to other parts of what you do or need to do can open up other ways to improve. Also share your thoughts on what you believe are the levels you need to achieve with your peers, so they can keep you accountable and maybe help improve things. They may offer sound advice on areas you don't have knowledge about. Benchmarking or measuring is a very important part of understanding what adjustments you may need to make.

BODY LANGUAGE

A great sales agent understands body language. I can't tell you how to read body language but I can make you very aware you must understand it. There are many quality books on the subject.

You must be aware that people are reading your body language too, during meetings, presentations, etc. We can all tell when someone is interested in us. Some call it gut feel but most of the time it is a result of viewing other people's body language. Put this on your 'things to do' list and read up on the subject. You do not have to be an expert but just developing an understanding of the basics will help you no end.

Communication has a number of parts and body language is one of them. Think about it the next time you are speaking with someone you have just met. You will come away with an impression of them and part of that impression will not come from the words they have spoken it will be from the body language you have read without knowing it.

Next time you are in a sales meeting watch the others in the room carefully. How do they react physically to what is happening in the room? As a kid I used watch people on the bus and train on the way to school. It was a lot of fun working out what was really happening with people on the train. You can learn a lot through observation and that is what body language is all about.

BUYERS ARE NOT LIARS

I recalled earlier the phrase "buyers are liars", that I heard when I attended my first course at the real estate institute. What a load of crap! This expression was created by the bad agents who could not qualify potential buyers. Yes, there are people who have difficulty deciding what they want but as an agent if you ask the right questions you then qualify buyers correctly and decide whether to invest more time with them or not. The bad agents don't know how to qualify and therefore waste time with unqualified buyers. Is that the buyer's fault?

You must remember that there are two sides to a transaction and one side is the buyer – without whom you cannot complete a sale. In many markets throughout Australia, buyers have to sell their property first to be able to purchase another, irrespective of whether they are upsizing or downgrading. In fact, in some areas it can be 60 per cent of buyers who need to sell first before they can buy. Do you think they might just be looking for an agent to sell their home as well?

Looking to buy a home can be very frustrating for families especially if both parents work, they still have all the other commitments that come with having a family. So, if you think about it, if you were a family that wanted to move but were struggling with time, wouldn't it be great to find an agent who really understood how your time was limited? Someone who listened and only showed you properties that really suited your needs? Would you stay loyal? I think so.

Many agents have a two-minute conversation over the phone with a buyer and think they know their needs. Well you might get lucky, but I think if you truly looked into their needs and made an appointment to go to their home, looked at what they are used to and got a better understanding of their taste, I believe the results would be far better.

Very few buyers are made to feel important by agents. There are some smart agents in the field who have focused on buyers in recent years with outstanding results. Top agents with personal assistants have identified this market and have really found a gold mine of opportunity. The have had their personal assistants focus on servicing these people which has led to listings that they would not normally get – they also proved to be a great source of referral business.

If you believe buyers are liars you are right and if you believe they are an untapped resource for business you are also right!

That's why we include this discussion on buyers in the selling chapter – because buyers increase your sales!

LOOK THROUGH THE CONSUMER'S EYES

As a result of being in the industry for years, many agents forget what it is like to be the client. Agents forget how an owner feels when they first put their home on the market and at times how difficult it is to make that decision. Clients want to feel understood and to do that you must imagine in your mind how they feel and how what you say affects them.

Many sales people forget that selling your home is not something most people do every day and it's the same for the buyer. They are often nervous about making the decision to buy. They need to be supported while making the buying decision, as well as afterwards. A good agent will guide them through to settlement.

As we do it every day, at times we become a little too smart with people and forget that quite often they really don't understand the process. Never assume that a buyer or seller fully understands the process. Many will feel uncomfortable telling the agent that for fear of appearing foolish. If you want to grow your network and receive referrals, master the art of looking at the situation through the client's eyes. You will make fewer mistakes in managing the people involved and develop a reputation for being an agent who cares and listens.

When you make the people you deal with feel important, they will be clients for life not just one transaction. The next sale you make, imagine you are outside the deal and in your mind look back at it and see it from an outsider's point of view. How did you deal with the sale? See in your mind how each person in the transaction felt based on how much experience they have had in dealing with such a transaction. Take it a step further and ask the people involved how they felt and what they believed would have made the experience better from their point of view. This view may be very different to what you thought so you can learn from it for the future.

PRODUCTIVE VS BUSY

As I speak with sales people on a day-to-day basis, I ask the normal question "how are things going?" and the standard answer is "busy".

Busy doing what? This is the first thing that pops into my mind when I hear this statement. As you are now well aware, I am very much into measuring performance and I have never written a business plan that said just be busy. I have listed actions, targets, things that I need to learn, habits I need to address and assistance that I may need but I never write busy.

Many agents are so busy being busy they don't have time to be productive. Controlling your actions, ensuring they are in line with what you are required to do to achieve your goals is productive not busy.

We are judged by results, not by how busy we are. It is possible to walk into a shoe-manufacturing factory and find people busy and there still could be shoes not being produced. There has to be someone doing the basics of producing the shoes – that is, putting them together and ensuring the basic actions are occurring – to get a result.

We live a world of numbers and numbers are very powerful. They don't lie but people do and we can justify anything if we talk long enough. You need to measure your productivity not how busy you are. Find a system of measurement and make yourself accountable.

BE A GREAT MARKETER

There are two major parts to what an agent does.

1. You need to be great marketer
2. You need to be a good negotiator.

We'll look at marketing here first.

Both your own personal marketing and the marketing of your properties need to stand out from the crowd. You need to create a system of marketing that makes you easily recognisable. It needs to be quality marketing at every level, right down to the type of paper you use in your brochures. I see hundreds of agents produce marketing pieces that have been poorly-written and presented, photocopied badly and which are crooked and have faded.

You need to create a marketing campaign so that you have a sequence of events you can measure and cost to determine its effectiveness. That way you can repeat the sequence in the future if it is successful.

Marketing does not have to be expensive. You may simply have a basic newsletter that is mailed directly to your database of people on a regular basis. Many agents sponsor a local sporting club at a low cost and attend their games regularly. My business supports a number of schools and sporting clubs and one thing that I have found is that you need to also have some personal involvement to get the best results.

The local high school I sponsor is attended by my daughters. At the year twelve graduation each year I present a book as an award to the students. The real cost is $50 and two hours of my time and in return the school prints my company name and logo in their newsletter and the program for the night. I speak in front of over 500 people that evening. How effective is that?

I also speak at a number of other events including one at the local technical college once a year which runs a selling unit as part of one of their courses. At this event, I am invited to talk for an hour about what I have experienced, and naturally I mention my company. Every year we make at least two sales as a result of that talk.

In your marketing, have interesting things to relate, not only about yourself but also about real estate in general. Short sharp messages are good. Photos of you receiving awards or giving them are very effective. Photos of you with famous people are excellent. You need to make yourself stand out from the crowd. 'Aditorials', that is, when you buy space in the local paper and write your own articles are very effective and stamp you as the local expert. Avoid sounding like everyone else. It may be worth talking to a marketing company to help you along with ideas if this is not what you are good at.

YOU NEED TO BE A GREAT NEGOTIATOR

As mentioned above, a great agent needs to be a very good negotiator. This skill is easy to learn but many people are scared to be negotiators, or they are really bad at it. This is why our industry exists because most people are poor negotiators.

Sales people who get great results are the ones who get the business. Agents who are able to work with all parties and get them to agree to price and conditions get the referrals.

As an owner, would you refer business to someone who poorly negotiated the sale of your home? Being able to use good scripting during the transaction is very important as is knowing what to say at the right moment.

An example would be asking a buyer, "Is this your best offer?" Often the response is "Yes." But the next question is the big one. "So, if the owner wanted a little bit more would you walk away?" The other question could be rephrased to something like, "If another buyer wanted to make an offer would you like to know, so that you could reconsider the amount you have offered?"

Great negotiators get the best fees because they know how to close on higher fees and in most cases get the best net result for their clients. Sloppy negotiators lose owners millions of dollars every year.

Who pays your fee? The owner. So if you were an owner and you had an agent working for you, what would you want? I know – the best result. And the only way that can happen is if the agent is a great negotiator.

To be a great negotiator you need to be able to look at the deal from all angles and you don't get emotionally involved in the transaction. In difficult deals, there has to be a strong person involved holding everyone together, listening and organising everyone but most importantly controlling the transaction.

If you receive an offer for an amount the owner wants but feel there is more the buyer might be prepared to pay, go and get it. The owner will love you and referrals will flow. The buyer will know how good you are and will certainly have you on their shopping list to sell their home later because they know you get every cent.

If your relationship is strong with owners you can be very open with them, especially if they have too high an expectation. Focus on their next step and how the current deal will allow that to happen.

I have found that by saying, "Will this amount get you to where you want to go?" I am able to close many owners who I have presented with an offer a little bit under their expectation. Buyers have an amount they would like to spend and an amount they can afford to spend. With owners there is an amount they would love to get and an amount they can afford to accept. Sales people who can negotiate build a great reputation that breeds referral business.

There are many agents who take panic into a negotiation and that is often through their own fear of not closing the deal. Or they may simply be trying too hard, which may sound a little strange. Perfectionists can struggle in negotiations at times because they don't always go quite the way you expect.

An example of this is when you go to a person's home to write the offer and they have the family adviser there as well. You may not feel in control in this environment. This can be very important as you need to be balanced. I personally never had too many issues with this, as I have a pretty solid procedure in terms of how I approach the writing of an offer. This came after years of experience, as it will with you. I know of agents who make the buyer come to them and do this part of the process in their own office environment. This isn't bad practice but it is not always practical.

If you are nervous, your panic can be transferred to your owners when you present the offer and that is one of the most dangerous things that can happen. A controlled environment is essential, as it can be an emotional time for a million different reasons. Imagine you have lived in your home for 30 years or 50 years. You are finally saying goodbye to a home you love and have enjoyed for decades. You have to get the vendors to focus on their next life step or goal, which will guide them towards making the right decision. Owners' panic can be transferred to you as well so keep calm throughout.

You can scream later when you're by yourself – trust me I have done that more than once.

Smiles help you close more deals than frowns.

BEWARE THE ANGER

There will be times if you work in sales when the ugly beast of anger will emerge. Be careful, anger in a client is very damaging to any negotiation, but anger in the mind or heart of the agent can be even more damaging. Agents are tested regularly and anger can be an exhausting emotion that can have a serious effect on your ability to produce results.

Owners, tenants and other agents will test you on a regular basis so you need to be strong. You need to be able turn the negative into a positive. You don't have to be an experienced agent to do this. The ability to do this comes from within. It is a discipline that you need to have to be successful. There will be times when you want to walk away and at times I know I have, but to come through these times and succeed is very fulfilling.

Anger is a very powerful emotion, you need to be able to turn it around and use that energy in the right direction, to focus on results. If you are able to think your way through a situation and remain patient and in control, you will succeed.

How many of us have said something in an emotional state and later regretted it? In negotiations or in sales you need to use this energy to drive you, not hinder you as many do. Beware the beast and turn it into a positive that can drive not destroy you.

8. KEYS TO
LONG-LASTING SUCCESS

n this chapter, now that we have discussed the six steps to real
estate success, I want to share with you other lessons I have
learned from my extensive experience in real estate.

First of all, I want to talk about balance.

BALANCE

Unless there is a balance between you, your family and your
personal life then there will be an imbalance in your business life
and vice versa. I know far too many agents who put business before
family and their own needs with devastating results. You have only
one opportunity to be at a child's fifth birthday or your daughter's
graduation. You cannot reschedule these things but you can most
of the time reschedule your business appointments.

At times, life flies by and the family events are what you look
back on later in life, not the deals you have made. I personally have

four daughters and that can keep a parent pretty busy just by itself, let alone owning a company too. I attend all my daughters' major events and regularly enjoy their achievements with them, as they do with me. It's not unusual to see my children at various events I have in my own business and training company.

Family comes first, second and third in my life and so should your family for you. You may not be married with kids, but you still need to have time for yourself and time to spend with friends to help recharge the batteries.

There has to be a purpose to what you do. In other words, there has to be a world outside of work that benefits or encourages you to be the best you can be in the field of sales. You have to be fulfilled in and out of work. Try to find interests that are not work-related, things that you enjoy and that allow you to switch off.

Don't let the frustrations of work interfere with your home life. To perform at the highest level at work you need to be complete in your life and that means to have all parts of your life under control and running smoothly so you can focus on what is important to you.

Several months ago I started receiving regular massages, which is something I had earlier thought unnecessary. My wife gave me a voucher to have a massage, she must have sensed I needed to get my body and mind more relaxed to deal with some of the extra projects I had taken on. I needed to relieve some of the extra tension that was building up and she had noticed this. I must admit it was the best thing anyone could have done for me. I was able to deal with things better and felt better within myself afterwards. Now I have committed to having a weekly or fortnightly massage.

I was talking with my daughter Nicole (who was 15 years old at the time) about material things. As we all know, at that age children start seeing things a little differently. I told her someone told me a long time ago that when your life is coming to an end you look back and all you have are memories. Your family only have their memories of you too. So you don't want to be saying, "I wish I had seen more of my friends and family." And you don't want your family and friends saying, "I can't remember much about him because he was always at work". Most clients understand you have other needs outside of work and in fact many respect people who can balance work and family.

SOMETIMES YOU HAVE TO PUT YOURSELF FIRST

In my life, as I imagine happens in yours, I have put other people ahead of myself and in the end this has backfired. In sales and in life, we far too regularly think we are helping someone when in reality we end up hurting ourselves, our family and friends.

I know in my life I got to the stage where I was cancelling more appointments with my family and friends than I kept, yet in business it was the opposite.

You need to take care of yourself first, which is the opposite to what we are taught growing up. Some people see taking care of themselves first as being selfish, but there are many times when you just have to.

Time management is one of the cornerstones of taking care of yourself first. When you can, get people to work around you. I don't know about you, but I have cancelled far too many gym sessions which in the end led to me not going at all and becoming unfit again!

All I am saying is make sure you do the important things first in your life. If you don't, you will never do the things that are meaningful for the people you care for and love – your family and friends.

You need to be fit and healthy and have time for yourself so that you can have the energy to do all the other things in your life.

Many people have a list of things they would love to do but never get around to. A classic example is the kayak I bought one year. I had wanted one for as long as I could remember. We live not far from the river and I enjoy a paddle because it helps me switch off. But that kayak just simply sat in my shed for four years – it only went in the water twice in that time. Every week I would say to myself, "Got to get out there in the summer". Yet every weekend I didn't take the kayak out. Now I look back and think what the hell did I really do? I know I didn't do the one thing I had really wanted to do.

Many of us spend far too much time pleasing others and not ourselves. This seems pretty foolish to me, what do you think? So the next time something pops up that isn't in line with your goals, consider carefully whether the real value is there for you, the person doing it.

Quite often, you find better ways to help others. But you still need to understand that investing time in yourself is also a true investment and the rest of the world will benefit more if you look after yourself.

WHEN YOU'RE ON TOP HOW DO YOU STAY THERE?

This is a question I often ask top agents. The answers are many and varied but one consistent theme comes through: "Keep in contact with your network".

This is something that those who stay on top do day in, day out. Many agents have what I call 'moments of glory' where they have a great month and then fade away for another three and then pop up again. They're usually in more of a survival mode, rather than in a career or business mode. Top agents understand how they arrived at their success – what got them there. They have a good grasp of the basics of business planning and ensure they keep their numbers at a level consistently, not just every now and then.

Elite athletes talk about personal bests (PBs) and I have discovered top agents do the same. They don't compete with others but with themselves, aiming to improve their performance in various aspects of their business. Top agents don't look for magic wands to fix their performance, they look at what they are doing to make themselves accountable and aim to improve their actions which create success. All top performers attend a lot of training because they are looking for better or simpler ways to do business or just to remind themselves of what they have stopped doing.

Surroundings are very important. You won't find outstanding performers hanging around the coffee pot whingeing about the boss and talking about how hard the market is. That's where you will find plenty of the low performers, blaming the world for the vendor or the contract that is driving them crazy. We all have issues, even the top sales people, but instead of talking they are doing; and it is in the doing that the seeds of greatness grow. Top performers know this and that is why they stay on top!

Goals drive your willingness to do what needs to be done. You will find top performers are very goal-focused. To be one of the best, you need to be fluid enough to be able to change with the times, the market and the challenges it may present to you.

CHANGE

Change is simply part of life. In this book, I talk a lot about keeping up with things and maintaining focus. Real estate has had some dramatic changes over my time in the industry.

The internet has probably been the most influential change to date. Markets change, technology changes and people's needs change, so your ability to read this change is very important. Having that ability to handle change, or finding people who can do this for you, is an important cornerstone to your future.

Many things I did in the early days of my career, I still do but I do them differently in some ways. One example is the way you greet people. You can be slightly more casual these days but you still need to be respectful. The consumers are far more educated as they can do more research on line than ever before – so agents need to be more prepared too.

Clients challenge fees more often, so you need to be able to justify your costs and explain the service and results they are paying for. You then have to prove your worth. Bank policies change all the time too, on what they will lend. So you need to have a great broker to be able to refer clients to for finance.

There are numerous government schemes around for potential buyers as well. In the early days, when I started, no one wanted building inspections, now they want them all the time, the list goes on and will get longer in the future. So embrace change as a friend not an enemy. I find that the agents who want the good old days to come back struggle with the reality of today. You need to be ahead of the game not behind, as you will never catch up, and there is nothing worse than feeling you are chasing all the time.

HAVE A GREAT PERSONAL ASSISTANT

Many highly successful sales people have a personal assistant and in some cases a number of assistants.

Why would you have an assistant?

As your business develops and you become busier, it will become more and more difficult to be able to do all that is necessary for your clients, as well as maintaining your prospecting activities – not to mention finding that balance we have just discussed between your personal and business life.

When deciding to have an assistant, you have to first fully understand why you want to have one. That is, you have to mentally be ready to share the responsibility of what you do. That means letting go of some of the basic tasks and being happy to admit there are things you are better having some one else do.

A lot of agents start with an administration assistant and later add a selling agent who also assists with prospecting, home opens and showing homes. Some agents don't stop at one assistant, recently I heard the term EBU (effective business unit) which was used to describe a sales person and his team of assistants.

It is the sales person who generally employs these assistants, not the company they work for. So if you decide to appoint an assistant you need to learn new leadership and management skills. You need to create a system and have clear objectives for your team. It is a good idea to speak with someone who has already done this and learn from their experience.

There may be courses available for your newly-appointed assistant to attend to get some training in the role.

There are a number of companies throughout Australia who put on cadets who work with experienced people for a year or two and then become sales people themselves later. Some stay as assistants, as they enjoy working in that position better and prefer not to take the next step.

I know of agents who have started with an assistant from day one and it has been very successful but you truly need to do your homework first. You must be able to afford to take someone on from the outset and have a clear idea of what support you need.

For the top sales people, having an assistant enables them to focus on the high-dollar producing tasks, for example the appraisals; and there will be more to do because of the leads generated your assistant(s). Much of the background work for your appointments will be done by your assistant so you will be able to concentrate on giving a quality presentation.

Taking on an assistant is something I would recommend the entrepreneur-minded agents to consider as part of their planning to be a top agent.

Three years ago I had one staff member, Charmaine, join me as my personal assistant and she has made an enormous difference to my personal productivity. She has allowed me to focus on what I do best, and the tasks I did averagely, she does brilliantly. My memory is better as she regularly reminds me of what I should have completed and this keeps me on track.

My assistant is someone I can share my thoughts with and she often provides support to me at times and inspires me to tackle the tough jobs.

We were fortunate to have the opportunity to spend a day with a gentleman called John McGrath – a highly successful agent and business person in Sydney and his assist Sue-Ellen. Spending that day watching them work together was a privilege. John is a very busy man and Sue-Ellen's ability to keep John on track with his appointments and take care of the background work was incredible to watch. John is a true professional and if you ever have the opportunity to listen to him speak I would thoroughly recommend it.

Spending that day with John McGrath was one of the break-throughs in my career – it got me organised! Upon our return to Perth, Charmaine and I sat and discussed what we had witnessed and today we still benchmark against that day. It was a very motivating experience to watch elite business people doing what they do best and that memory will live with me, and I believe Charmaine, for a long, long time. Thanks John and Sue-Ellen.

THE FOUR SEASONS

When you have been in real estate for some time, you will discover there are cycles the market goes through. Many things will influence markets, such as the Global Financial Crisis (GFC) in recent years.

In Australia, we weren't affected as badly as the rest of the world by the GFC, in fact in my part of Australia (in Western Australia) we didn't experience as much pain as other parts of the country. There was some drop off in prices but in general property values didn't fall dramatically. In my opinion, the Australian recession in the early 1990s was far worse but for many it was an excuse not to do well.

As well as these big global or national cycles, there are the four seasons. These four seasons are consistent market conditions that

I have experienced and they have an effect on an agent's income. Understand these seasons and you will improve your chances of success.

Everyone wants their income to increase every year – or at least stay at a level that they are happy with. But this achievement is quite rare because many agents aren't prepared for all the four seasons that are presented to them. Generally they do not adjust their business plans and strategies accordingly to the conditions of the season they are in.

I refer to the four selling seasons in the same terms as the seasons of the year, the main difference is the real estate seasons last for different lengths of time.

Spring

Spring is the season when people talk about romance. It is the season when temperatures are more pleasant. You are coming out of winter so spring seems far more comfortable.

For an agent, it seems as if all the work you've done in the darker hours of winter are starting to come together. Things feel fresh, everyone's happy – including the boss – because he or she sees new things happening as well. Spring can be the time when you feel invincible!

But be careful that it doesn't become the time when you stop doing the things that work well for you – finding buyers and sellers – because spring is also the season when we can all get a bit lazy. There's the risk that you run off and do things that don't maintain your presence in the market. Instead, you make plans for other things (which is OK but you need to make sure they are in balance).

Spring lasts for as long as you have a balance between your stock and buyer inquiry levels. For some agents this can run for a long time. For others who start out in spring with not much stock, they won't attract enough interest to generate business so they won't even experience the spring that the average agent will experience. For them it will be a very short period and may only come when a boom occurs – and even then they may only see it, not really experience it. Booms are not what we sit around waiting for, we need to maintain our numbers so we have a flow of potential buyers and sellers in our database so our spring can last longer.

Summer

Summer follows spring and this is the time to still enjoy the sunshine but it can start to become heated, representing a shift in the market. Buyer frenzy may occur, especially in boom times. You may find yourself fighting for listings and having to tighten your fees. You could be doing more work for less pay.

So now you are working harder and more effort is needed but the results are the same. In some cases, business starts to drop off but you still feel everything is not too bad. Every now and then you become uncomfortable because the heat does hit you a bit and you think "Gee, I'll be glad when things cool off."

However tempting it may be, you cannot cool off too much. You simply can't justify dropping activities and winding things back because the heat is on. You may have let too much slip in the spring and now be chasing business which is making you feel too hot – with all that extra effort necessary to get things back in balance.

Yes markets can slow in the summer too and if you haven't adjusted to the heat this will hit you like a brick. At this stage you are chasing even more buyers and listings and getting even hotter under the collar.

Autumn

Autumn arrives after summer and this is the season when you still have a few warm days but mostly the days are cooler. Business tends to change a bit too, moving from hot to cool and even to wet at times!

Some of your efforts pay off in this period and this can lead to a false sense of security. You may start thinking that maybe spring is back. You can be quite forgiving to yourself, even pat yourself on the back saying "Hey, well done you have got through summer without too much damage."

As autumn comes on, you will start to see further cooling. Less seems to be happening but the better times are still in your mind, they haven't gone yet. You think, "well, it is only one cool day it will be better tomorrow." But thinking this rather than doing more is now the problem. You can fall into a pattern of doing less which leads to less results which are possibly even more random. The results, like the season you are in, are a bit hot and cold and as each day goes by the temperature seems to fall further.

Winter

Winter is most people's least favourite season and it can be this way in real estate too. You have been feeling the cold coming over autumn. Your listings are getting fewer and the number of buyer inquiries has reduced. You may still have what you think are good listing numbers, but buyer confidence may be down.

Your stock is now stale as you hold listings for longer and the owners are starting to ask more questions. All of a sudden it feels as if the property prices have come off and to be honest you feel sick in the stomach. You don't want to tell the owners because of all the promises you made when you listed their property.

It is easy to be negative because others in the industry are not enjoying the cold. Together you cuddle up to the weaker agents to keep warm, deep in the bullshit of blaming the market!

You wish you hadn't made the promises you had made and wonder why you took on some of the listings that are causing you angst. Buyers have sensed they are more in control and therefore become more annoying. You start thinking of them as smart arses (and the list goes on).

What has really happened is that your prospecting numbers have been slow because you are hoping your current stock will sell, but you now wish you had some fresh stock. You are represented in the marketplace with poor, stale stock and no fresh inquiries to get things kick-started. It is during winter that many retreat, desperate to find warmth.

Winter like all the seasons lasts as long as you allow it to. The change in buyer inquiry levels or owners wanting to negotiate commissions is determined by how much presence you have in the market place and agents forget this. When you have stock flowing in you are more confident and you don't have to grovel to get business. Business continues to flow as people see you as active. If buyer activity slows down, but you have more stock and fresh stock still flowing in, you will attract whoever is out there – you are a magnet with stock. Let the others have the over-priced and low commission stuff so that you can flourish, spending more time with genuine sellers.

As I have said, the seasons are related 100 per cent to your effort and consistency throughout the year. Your aim is make spring permanent. Yes, you will get days that have all the seasons appear but the less wanted seasons only pop up for a day rather than months. I will take that any time.

New fresh stock will get you through any season.

THIS IS NOT A PART-TIME JOB!!!

There are some people who think that they can be a successful real estate agent working part time. This is rubbish. You cannot deliver service to a client part time. You can't say to a person, "look I will sell your home when I have time after I finish my other job."

The owner is paying a good fee for good service. The fee should reflect the service level. Real estate is not a fill-in position. You are dealing with people's largest assets and this needs focus and commitment to get the best results. For anyone who is thinking of coming into the industry part time you will be wasting your time and that of others.

Having said all that, there are some agents who attend offices full time but who are only committed part time. By this I mean there are some who think they are working the hours but truly aren't. They have no focus, they don't do the extra for the clients. They don't have a business plan or a direction and survive from sale to sale – many offices have this type of agent. I have seen offices that have a team of ten but probably only have three producing any results, the others are just hanging in. This is not the type of office you want to be involved in.

There are many agents who have little guidance in the beginning and develop poor habits which stay with them their whole careers. They are generally poor time managers and spend all day doing something that would take a true professional ten minutes to do.

There was a stage in my own career when I believe I moved from being a part-timer to a true professional. That happened when I decided to put in place an ideal week and focus on set activities. I worked on these and developed my skills, fine-tuning them on a regular basis. Rather than being random, on a day-to-day basis my outcomes became more predictable and so did my income. I focused on what I should be doing on a consistent basis before I tried different things.

If you are forever switching and changing it means you're only really trying things in a part-time fashion. You're not hanging in for the better results, just looking for quick fixes and the longer you are in any occupation you learn that these don't work.

Many sales people with a part-time mentality do what I call 'rainbow chase'. They are always looking for the rainbow, with the pot of gold at the end of it. We know there are no rainbows, only results as a by-product of focus on great service.

KNOWLEDGE IS POWER

You don't have to be an expert in everything but it's important to know how to find out things when the need arises. To have an opinion you need to have experience and you get this by researching and observing what is happening around you.

Read what is happening in your local area in the papers or attend council meetings. Meet the local people who will be happy to share with you what is happening in your area of influence.

The internet is now a very powerful tool for finding things out faster but at times there is almost too much information. So stick to what you really need to know. In other words, find out only what is useful information.

Confidence is a big by-product of knowledge. You don't need to know everything just have an understanding of what is going on in your area and industry.

Establish a knowledge network. It can be very effective, saving you hours of research. For example, if you have never done a subdivision or development, meet someone who has and generally they will help you sharing their experiences. The longer I am on this planet the more I become aware of what I don't know but I have discovered my network for finding out things is very, very powerful. Feed your network and it will feed you.

ATTEND ALL THE TRAINING

Many agents are poorly trained. They have simply received very little training. Training is something you always need to invest in. Successful people always attend training regularly. It helps you to track trends and also assists you with focusing on what really works. There are many quality trainers in the field and I would recommend you attend at least three sessions a year, outside of your office environment, so you can cast a wider net for knowledge.

Sometimes you just need a kick in the pants to get back to basics; other times training may refresh your outlook on things in general. I suggest that you mix your training up if you can. There are many quality DVDs and CDs you can purchase and listen to in your car or watch at home or in the office.

Everyone needs a lift at times. I know I have and I consider myself a very focused, positive and determined person but I still need fine-tuning. Top sales people are learners. They continue to succeed because they change with markets when they have to, they are very in tune with new ideas and also find ways to improve on basics at a higher level.

You need to have a training calender for the year and a budget to cover the associated costs. Too many people say they cannot afford it, I say they can't afford not to afford it.

There is so much information available these days on the internet. Also if you ever have the opportunity to have lunch with a top producer do it, and pay for the lunch! There have been times I have learnt more over a coffee with a top producer than I have from attending seminars, but you do have to have a healthy diet of both.

By the way, not all training has to be real estate focused. As I have mentioned, you need balance and that might be in other areas of your life as well, not just in your sales career. You may attend training just for your own general interest which helps you switch off for a few hours. My main point is don't turn off from new experiences and views that can help you progress in all areas of your life.

One of the advantages I have found over the years by attending conferences is that they enable me to network with similar-minded people. There have been times I have learnt more in the lunch break at one of these conferences than from the speakers.

Sharing experiences with others of similar interests can be a huge learning experience, and it allows you to develop relationships for the future and sometimes for life.

Get out there and experience as much as you can. Sometimes by simply committing to something quite often, I have found I've also got some good time for reflection.

MANY OF THE ANSWERS ARE AROUND YOU

I personally have travelled far and wide looking at real estate practices and sales teams searching for the magic formula. The truth is there is no magic formula that will make you a success over night.

Recently I travelled to the United States to attend the National Realtors Conference – there were 20,000 agents there, and 600 exhibitors. The conference went for four days and was full on. I spoke with agents from all over the world and the interesting thing was we all had the same issues. We all needed listings and buyers to buy them.

In the United States there are a large number of part-time people with a high failure rate and there is a large turnover in sales people as they leave the industry. Many operate on the desktop cost scenario which is where the sales person basically rents the desk and pays all the costs necessary to be in the industry. So therefore they are very individual in the way they work and have a general scatter-gun approach to marketing. This is great for the advertising companies but not for the sales person.

Many sales people are poorly educated, their overall results are very low and the number of private sales is high.

I travelled around the world to discover that many of the best agents are in my own backyard. Within a sales team there are things you can observe and learn from by simply listening. As I suggested earlier, take a top producer out for lunch then learn from their experience. Find out where the best agents go, what functions they attend, and hang around them. You will learn if you network.

Also you learn by keeping accurate records of what does and does not work for you. Ask the public what they want from an agent. Ask people you know what their experiences have been. Find out what they would ask an agent and how they would find one if they were looking to sell their property. Research what clues are left around by the top agents in your area, e.g. what type of personal marketing do they do, what organisations do they belong to. There is plenty you can find out. Then find a way to do better. It does not take a lot. Look in your backyard first before you look outside to help develop your ideas.

FEAR IS YOUR FRIEND

I have a belief that fear is a friend. This may surprise you but you need courage to succeed in sales. Fear is a great motivator as it increases your awareness of what is happening. Also, if you feel fear that suggests what you are doing means something to you and that is very important.

Even after 28 years in the industry, when I'm presenting to people I feel that little knot in my stomach which reminds me of the things I should be doing and that this appointment that I am attending still has meaning. Fear keeps us on our toes, our senses are at a higher level which I think is a good thing.

You will feel calmer as your career grows but there will always be a tough question or two that you need to deal with. There will always be that presentation that you really want to close that creates a bit of fear within but it is healthy to enjoy it and use it to motivate not deflate you.

Sales people often go into the unknown and when they do so they can do their best work and learn. Going into the unknown is where the fun is and you should encourage yourself to push the boundaries. As human beings we need to have experiences that keep us fresh and looking forward. Far too many people are experts in a world that no longer exists. In sales and in life you can't afford to be one of these, either emotionally or financially.

When fear appears, there are many who are blinded by it to the extent they cannot see what is around them. Just like when my wife asks me to look for the salt in the pantry and I advise her there is none. She replies that it is there and it is in the spot it always has been for the last five years. Yet I can't see it. My fear of not knowing or seeing it kicks in and so I am looking and not seeing it anywhere. My heart rate is going up and I don't want to feel embarrassed. I just cannot find the bloody salt!

My wife asks again, have I found it, and now I am in the fight or flight stage. My heart rate is up and I'm feeling as if I am blind. I am now certain there is no salt in the pantry. She walks over calmly to me and reaches to the shelf and immediately places her hand on the salt and gives it to me with a smile on her face.

My heart is still racing and I start to feel a little bit angry that within a second she has found what I couldn't. "Open your eyes," she says.

Now why does this happen? Good question.

In my opinion there are two types of fear. There is the fear that you can embrace and use to take you to new levels, and there is fear that has built up from past mistakes and your past experiences, which you have carried forward with you. The latter can make you blind to everything around you. You expect the same bad outcome as before, and therefore a fear builds inside of you similar to what happened to me when I couldn't find the salt, because at some stage I had annoyed my wife or others before.

I link a bad personal outcome or feeling to a ghost I have brought forward which helps present the fear in my mind and body again, without me realising it. This happens to many, many sales people who bring past bad sales experiences forward with them. It may be a previous bad experience they had when they were prospecting. Perhaps when they had been telephone prospecting, someone had got aggressive with them so they expect this could happen again in the future and it puts them off.

If you expect failure the chances are you will get what you expect. Let go of the ghosts and look forward to the new experiences ahead and accept that fear is a friend that can help. You can control it and use it to your benefit. Fear is not always about scary monsters.

THE MARKET IS IN YOUR HEAD

This is one of the first bits of advice I got when I started in real estate. It was given to me from my first principal Dave Fisher at Roy Weston in Midland, way back in 1987. Dave was a pretty direct type of guy. There were no shades of grey with Dave but he did have a good heart and if he could pass on knowledge that he thought would benefit you he would. This bit of advice "the market is in your head," has always stuck with me. I have heard it said many times since and it is the most logical thing a senior manager has shared with me.

I have seen sales people flourish in all sorts of markets that have been described as difficult. They have still made great sales and earned excellent incomes. I have seen other sales people make no sales in a so-called boom.

The ability to see opportunity in any market is purely in your head – yes, right between your ears. If sales are slower than normal look for what can improve:

- Are your listing prices too high?
- Do you have the right stock to attract interest?
- Are your owners really motived to sell?
- Are you really doing what is required to close the sales?
- Have you let basics slip, e.g. your prospecting efforts?

The list could go on for pages but in your head you decide whether to search for answers or not – persist or give up.

It's funny but I have seen new sales people come on board and make sales in their first weeks. They think it is easy but then sales drop right off because they are not prepared to give the commitment that comes from how you think. It is easy to find other lazy people to justify your poor habits but it takes a real professional to challenge themselves and not accept the poor habits.

There are always people looking to sell, buy, lease or invest in real estate, you just have to find them first. You need to hunt all the time and that means you need to be alert to the opportunities presented to you. Feeling organised is in your head. It is your perception of what is organised and whether you are capable of being that way or not. Every day you will receive "no's" from people. That is part of life. It is how you internalise the "no's" that determines your next action.

We tend to over-complicate things all the time, it's human nature. But if you keep your mind clear, you can see more and that is how to find business. It is all about clear focus. The market is always there because you are looking for it. Keep away from the doomsday people. I have met a million of them and they are a pain in the butt and energy-sappers.

If you hunt every day for opportunity it will present itself. Success isn't for everyone because many don't have the persistence to look for it and the energy to take advantage of it when they have the chance to take it. The longer I have gone on in this journey of life, the more I have discovered how much real opportunity there is in world, whether it be real estate sales or purely the chance to grow as a person. Today is the doorway to tomorrow's opportunities and what actions we take today will guide us there. It's the belief that there is always something going to happen that keeps us going.

Here are some tips to keep you motivated in the marketplace:

- Take advice from someone who is making sales and listings not someone who isn't.
- Know that everyday people's lives change in ways that present opportunities to others.
- Seek and you shall find.
- Mistakes are opportunities to improve.
- Reflect what you desire.
- Don't wait for a perfect day, make today perfect.
- Every 'no' means you are closer to a 'yes'.

So what did I think when Dave shared his advice with me way back in 1987? I simply internalised that every day I expected something to happen, and if it didn't it meant I had to do more to make things happen. Every day I worked on ensuring the right stuff was going into my head. I wasn't clogging it full of stuff that would slow me down or that wasn't in line with my goals.

It is always up to me not others to find my success. You need to accept that because when you do it will set you free to achieve.

NEVER BE AFRAID TO ASK, ASK, ASK

Never fear asking. More mistakes have been made by people being too frightened to ask questions than anything else. Too much assumption happens in this world and at times this back fires. We are taught at a young age to be quiet and we take this through to adulthood. It can have a terrible impact on some people because it makes them fearful of asking questions.

Real estate is a questions game. The more we ask, the more opportunities we create for ourselves and our clients.

I am personally not a mind-reader so I ask lots of questions that help guide me on how I can build confidence in the other person to assure them that I am interested in them. Also it encourages the other person to do the same. Hopefully it opens up the communication to reach a much higher level.

I hear far too often, "If only I had known, I could have helped them". Well, you'll never know if you're too afraid to ask.

Selling real estate is not something owners do every day, so there will always be some natural fear around every transaction or potential to do business with someone. Remove the fear by asking questions. It also helps build the relationship and shows you care enough to ask people about their needs and about themselves.

MAKE THE BEST USE OF SOCIAL MEDIA

Social media is now very much a part of today's life and it will continue to evolve with new websites and networks popping up all the time. There is some great stuff on social media. It can be an invaluable tool for letting people know what you are doing, but there is also plenty of crap out there as well.

Every day I get an email or a call from someone telling me how to improve my Google search engine ratings. They all can't be right! And others tell me Facebook is the only way and the list goes on.

My advice is to have a budget for social media because it is just another way to diversify the advertising you are doing.

You have to be careful about what you put on social media because it is there forever. Social media has helped me get in contact with people I haven't spoken to for years and that has been great. But I have also seen how much pressure it can put on people when something is expressed poorly and there has been a misunderstanding over what has been said.

Be as current as you possibly can but be mindful how much effort and time you spend on social media because much of it can be a waste of time. Don't get me wrong, I have seen some great stuff but I think there are many other things you need to focus on early in your career, such as better systems and processes.

You can't ignore social media. It is part of the future. The internet has changed the world but you need to create the right impression in person as well as being interesting on the net.

It would be foolish to ignore social media but find a simple way to have yourself represented on it that is not costly and involves a minimum amount of your time. There will be plenty of people who will debate how you use social media but look at what you do and how you use it and decide from there. As I mentioned, things evolve all the time so you need to look at this area carefully and keep it simple so people can find you.

BE THE ENTREPRENEUR NOT THE ENTERTAINER

Over the years, since I started being a sales manager in 1989 and since I owned my own agency in 1999, I have discussed what makes a good sales person. What are their weaknesses and strengths?

I have also attended many real estate training sessions for managers and had endless discussions with other principals throughout Australia on this subject. I have heard many different ways to describe the performance of sales people – and some have not been very flattering, I can assure you.

Many of us don't like to use the word 'failing' because it is too broad a term. So we hear things like, "They just don't seem to be quite getting the results", or simply, "I can't understand what they aren't doing." For me as a manager I can only guide a sales person so far. I can't hold everyone's hand, so I need the individual to take responsibility for their outcomes. Rather than go through all the things I have seen that are wrong or potentially could go wrong, I think it is more useful to talk about mindsets. Hopefully you can understand my thoughts on this.

Most sales people fall into two main categories in terms of how they approach their career and what real service they present to the public. There are many views, so rather than present shades of grey I prefer to think that most fall into two colours, black or white. In my meetings with managers, I will listen to their description of how they communicate internally in the office and with clients. Quite often I then give them feedback on how I think they went in the field.

I describe a sales person as either an entertainer who will dance, sing and continue to do so as long as they can to keep the client smiling and not get in trouble.

Or I describe a sales person as an entrepreneur who is far more results-focused.

The entertainer will book extra ads for the owners, do extra opens, and promise more and more. Not because it is the best thing to do to get better results, more because it keeps everyone happy and not angry at them.

Don't get me wrong we need to do our best, but not just do anything that keeps people entertained. I have done it and I can tell you plenty of experienced people will admit they have done it too and in most cases they regret it. We don't do what we do for applause. Yes, we do want our clients to be happy but that is more about results than entertainment. The entertainer is very dangerous to themselves, their clients and the business they work for.

Now the entrepreneur thinks more about outcome than entertainment. In fact, he or she usually doesn't have time to entertain because they are onto the next step already. In my experience, direct honesty is more effective and achieves better results. The entrepreneur understands that effort needs to return profit. Creativity can be part of their world, similar in some ways at times to the entertainer, but they are still very results-focused.

They have less fear of what they do and understand risk is part of day-to-day business.

Now we can all drift between these two approaches but I find the sales people who are more of an entrepreneur do more than survive in real estate, they have a long, successful career. The entertainers eventually burn out or are seen through over time.

If you think about the people you have met over the years, the entertainers and those who you thought were a bit different and seemed to have a better focus, then you will probably agree the entrepreneurs get the job done better. Without them, life would be just full of theatre.

In my world I can't afford entertainers, I need to find people who make things happen. So I often ask my managers which category a sales person may sit in and whether we can get them to the right one. The hard thing is the entertainers are such nice people that managers struggle to tell them to change until it is too late.

Below are some definitions you may find interesting to support my point.

- **Entrepreneur** – "A person who sets up a business or businesses taking on financial risks in the hope of profit." *(Oxford Advanced Learners Dictionary)*

- **Entertainer** – "Someone whose job is to entertain people by singing, dancing, telling jokes, etc." *(Cambridge Advanced Learners Dictionary and Thesaurus)*

- **Salesperson** – "A person whose job is selling things in a shop directly to customers." *(Cambridge Advanced Learners Dictionary and Thesaurus)*

Keep these in mind when you are out in the field. Which will be the best type of agents to get the right results for your clients?

Be an entrepreneur, take charge of your career. Yes, our results bring happiness but let's help people take the next step in their lives. Let's not insult them by being an entertainer.

9. TAKE CONTROL OF
YOUR OWN FUTURE

Many people wait for things to happen rather than take control of their lives. Remember, things only change when you change.

I have a belief that you can only look forward, as I know of no one who has been able to change the past. In the future I hope to achieve many of the things that I have not done and fulfil the dreams I have.

You need each day to have something to look forward to, a purpose if you like. I know when my dad retired, he and many of his friends had worked hard for a long period of time (in Dad's case, 51 years as a baker). I can remember Dad sharing a beer with his mates, talking about retirement and how great it would be to be able to rest and no longer have to work. Interestingly, ten of Dad's friends died in the first year of their retirement.

I then remember talking to Dad and I recall him saying, "You work long hours for years son and then there is nothing. You don't have anything really to do that means anything". I believe many of Dad's friends died simply because they had no real focus for their future, nothing beyond the day they stopped working.

My mum died of cancer within nine months of my dad retiring. I was 19 years old and I watched my dad for the next 13 years of his life, sitting thinking about all the things he hadn't done. I said to myself I would never repeat that pattern in my life.

There are many people in society who let the government provide for them. They don't have much of a positive outlook on life and are very limited in what they will achieve. I am personally here to do as much as I can to have a positive influence on as many people as I can. That is my mission statement for life and I can't do that sitting on my bum.

Have great dreams, turn them into goals, create the steps that you have to take to achieve them and learn from the mistakes you make along the way. There are thousands of dream thieves out there – some are even your best friends – who really don't understand what it is like to achieve a goal. This is because they don't have them and so they don't want others to have them either.

You are the creator of your dreams and you are also the guardian of them. Share them with people who will give you the strength to make them a reality and do the same for them. As your dreams evolve, sometimes you have to break free from others to find extra strength and support to fulfil them.

There is no real excuse for not chasing your dreams and creating powerful goals. We all need a purpose and it is those who don't who float through life and one day wake up and say "what happened?"

No one will be interested in your future if you're not, why would they be? There are many who are scared of focused people because they do not understand the power of controlling their future by having goals which give them strength and focus and help control their future.

Life is very much about making decisions and delivering on those decisions. You will not always be right but you will get more right than you do wrong. You will have to trust me on that one. Try and see it for yourself.

I learn from my past but I don't live in it. I tried but I went backwards and became frustrated with myself time and time again. You have lived those past moments, you don't have to continually relive them.

Forgive yourself for past failures. I have made a million mistakes and I will make a million more but I look forward to the new ones because I will be learning from them and learning gives me fulfilment.

All of us have a purpose and we just have to live it. There are so many exciting things for us to look forward to. You might say that you don't like to take risks. The greatest risk is not trying. The world changes every day creating new waves for you to deal with. Ride these waves as often as you can and enjoy the experience. I truly hope that you look forward to your career and life with great excitement as I do and hopefully we can share the excitement together.

CONTROL YOUR ENVIRONMENT

It personally took me a while to understand how to control my environment when it was really something that is pretty simple. If you can get this early in your career it will be a huge benefit. Now some of this advice is really easy, other parts can be hard because it may mean a big change in what you do on a daily basis. Some of us are more social than others and some of us struggle to keep people out of our way in busy times.

There are a number of environments you need to control, let's take a look:

Home

Your home is one of the big ones. Your home environment affects how you start your day and how you finish your day. Now I am a parent of four kids, so my day can start out being quite hectic and finish the same way! Plus the transfer of pressure from your partner on their day can impact you big time.

Families work well in routines. Having certain routines with your family are very important – don't forget to include your pets as they are a big part of the family life as well in many cases.

Communication is vital within a family to ensure that routines are maintained and what needs to get done is done. Then everyone has to respect what each has to do in their day to make it happen. There will always be random things that pop up but that's simply a part of life. These challenges are not unique to you.

You usually go to work to support your family so they need to understand what you are trying to achieve. Share your goals with them and understand everyone else has goals too.

All families have their own unique culture and environment and you are a very big part of it. I have four daughters, three from my first marriage and one with my second wife. So I have had some interesting twists along the way in my attempt to maintain balance within my family environment. I have worked with my wife on what we need to focus on. At times it was tough but we have got through it as a family.

I have always had their support which makes things simpler. When I have had to work through the guilt of working extra hours at times, I have always known that my family understood why I was doing this and that is important.

Early in September 1999, within a space of two weeks, my wife and I received the keys to our new house which had just been built and we moved into our new home; we had our fourth daughter

Aimee; and started a new business all at the same time! My real estate office started that year with four staff. Today (in 2015) we have five outlets with two in the pipeline to open soon and we employ over 50 staff. So how we handled that couple of weeks has resulted in something worthwhile in many ways. Yes, it was tough but we worked together, understood what we needed to do and created the environment to make it happen.

Work

You spend more time at work at certain times than you do at home. What happens at work can impact on your home life, so you need to ensure you invest your day in the right activities and stay focused. This can be a massive challenge if you are not in an environment of encouragement and support.

Now don't confuse sitting around gas-bagging as being support. That is simply time-wasting. There will always be parts of the day lost to other people time-wasting but don't make it your time that's being wasted. Ensure what you are doing is in line with your goals. If it isn't, do something that is.

Keep away from the chook-feeders in the office. You know, the ones who seem to cluck all day about nothing and crap everywhere they go! You don't have time to solve everyone else's problems, you usually have enough of your own. Unless they want to give you a listing or a sale, the conversation isn't in line with what you are doing.

By the way, I am not saying be rude but let them know you have little time to spare as you have plenty on and you need to keep moving. Most people will respect that. People only behave around you in the way that you allow them to. So if they come and unload all their crap on you it is because at some stage you said it was OK. Chickens can't fly that well but eagles can so if you have to talk with anyone, talk with the eagles – they will help you fly.

Share your goals with your manager and make sure you create an environment of accountability to those goals with your manager. There can be office politics but don't get caught up in it. Be open and fair with your employer and you will find you will get the same in return in most cases.

Be part of the solution not the problem. Sometimes, unfortunately we can start out at the wrong place. Working for a good leader is important so ensure that if you need to move agencies to find one, you do so. It is your choice where to work.

Car

Your car is another environment where you spend a lot of time, so make it a place that helps you in more ways than just transporting you from A to B. Keep your car tidy and something to be proud of. It doesn't have to be an expensive car but something that is functional. You will need good air conditioning and something comfortable to drive.

Have the tools that you need in your car, such as a hands-free phone that uses blue tooth, and training CDs you listen to as you drive around, so you are learning as well as driving. Sometimes just having quality music playing keeps you either relaxed or pumped for your next appointment. Avoid the bad news on the radio and keep your mind clear.

A reliable car is essential in real estate to keep you on time and stress free. Your car is your mobile office, so have a kit in the car for back up information you may need when you're giving presentations to clients – always be prepared. It may be worth keeping a small pack containing a measuring tape and some cleaning stuff, just in case something happens at an open home and you need to freshen the air or wipe something clean.

Extended family and friends

Your extended family and friends make up a big part of your environment. These guys should have a good idea of what you do for a living and help you when you need a hug or a kick in the pants.

I have a couple of good school friends who I respect greatly and who add different things to my life. Peter, whom I grew up with, is a quiet guy who is always happy to have a chat and share the old times. He has a low pressure government job that would drive me crazy but it suits him. He thinks I am crazy for doing what I do, but he knows I am good at it and the same can be said about him. I hang out with Peter and his brother John every now and then and still catch up with their mum who now is in her eighties. She is Italian and her English has never been great. She has always been nice to me as I lost my mum when I was only 19. These people are important to me and have always made me feel welcome.

Another mate, Paul, I've known since we were in high school. He has been a success in commercial real estate and was the guy who had an influence on my interest in real estate. Paul tried to talk me into studying to be a valuer like him when we were younger. We have always kept in touch. He is pretty much a straight-shooter and has helped me refocus my efforts on more than one occasion.

I personally prefer a pretty no-bull-shit approach to achieving things and Paul has been a great supporter of that for me. I have a number of other great people who help me along as well. It is two-way traffic as I am there for them too. It is hard to get everything from one person and sometimes you have to step out of home to get the extra things you need.

Many years ago I worked for a guy called Bob Manning, for whom I have enormous respect. Bob was a great agent in his own right and a good person. He was always willing to help where he could. He was one of the fairest guys I have ever met – a true team player, which is something I have always respected. Although I have not worked with Bob for many years we still help each other when we can and he is always just a call away if I need some advice.

In recent years, I was fortunate enough to be in partnership with two great guys, Don Holmes and Peter Carter, who believed in an idea I had to create – Real Estate Plus. When we met, times were tough but they backed me and we were in partnership for 15 years. They have both been very successful in a number of other business they have built and I was fortunate enough to be able to have them as mentors. They challenged me regularly but at the same time they were very supportive. Today we are no longer partners as I own Real Estate Plus by myself but we are still good friends and hopefully will do other things together in the future.

Having these types of people in the background is very important but I still add people to this group all the time. Some people do drop off as well, not for bad reasons, they simply move out of your life. These people have encouraged me at times in ways you wouldn't believe. You don't have to live in other people's pockets to be real friends and respect each other.

Within yourself

You mustn't forget in your quiet moments that what you think and what you allow into your mind influences everything. So you need to be able to shift the bull dust from the truth in everything you do. To help others you have to take care of yourself first.

In your private moments it's important to use your time to its maximum effect. This is time for you to regenerate, refocus or whatever. Understanding what you really have in terms of skills and how to use them is essential for anyone doing anything. Understanding what help you need is just as important.

Knowledge is moving so fast, new technologies change every

minute of the day, so you can't keep up with everything. You need to find a network that can help you with technology and get them to do what you can't do. Also, don't let perfection get in the way of better. Don't be scared to challenge others to help you on your journey. Ultimately, you need to understand your direction and that your actions are always a reflection of what is happening within you whether you want them to be or not.

Control what you can control. You can't change the world alone but you can influence others to follow and they will if you have direction.

So who you surround yourself with is determined by you and no one else through your actions and what you seek.

CONCLUSION

I guess, getting back to what your thoughts are on what the market is and what you want in life as a whole will determine your outcomes more than anything else. It is human nature to take the easiest path but then you will end up where the others have been and may be and that is not what you really want.

You are in control whether you want to be or not. Acceptance of this helps you move forward.

A real estate career is an exciting journey and one that you will truly enjoy if you plan it to be that way. I have made many friends and developed many great relationships during my career and still look forward every day to going into the field with my staff. I do hope that you can feel the same way in 20 years' time and can talk about the successes and the enjoyment you have had in this exciting industry.

There will be days you would rather not have to go through but learn from them. I am a great believer in what you focus on you get.

Be a learner, expand your mind as often as you can and challenge yourself regularly. This will earn you respect from your peers.

Don't be scared to pat yourself on the back and I encourage you to share your experiences with others. Be a planner not a follower and create your own destiny.

While reading this book, you may have come across points that you feel you need to learn from, so go back and highlight them. Make yourself accountable to someone to work with on these areas. Decide on some action steps that you need to take and put a time line in place to reach them.

Get organised. Be disciplined to do the basic actions and things will flow. Persist in striving to fulfil your dream of being successful in this industry and it will happen. I hope this book has been a help. Thank you for your time and happy selling!